The Shropshire Way

A Walker's guide to the route
and matters of local interest.

Robert Kirk

Thornhill Press
24 Moorend Road
Cheltenham

ISBN 0 946328 05 6

The maps are based upon the relevant Ordnance Survey maps, with the permission of the Controller of H.M. Stationery Office, Crown Copyright reserved.

In the final printing stage, the strip maps on Page 67 & Page 78 were interchanged. The Author and Publisher regret this error and hope that it will not spoil readers' enjoyment of the guide.

On Page 8 Shropshire Rambling and Hill Walking Club should read Shrewsbury Rambling and Hill Walking Club.

CONTENTS

Front cover: Shropshire Way Fantasy. A whimsical composition showing
a footbridge over the River Roden, Hopesay Church and
Stokesay Castle Gatehouse, with the County boundary in
outline.

The Shropshire Way

FOREWORD

There is a great deal that one can say in praise of the Shropshire countryside. Most prominent are the wild, steep hills that stand like an advance guard ahead of the rugged Welsh uplands extending right across the western horizon. These fine remnants of a geologically ancient landscape overlook green and peaceful valleys and plains that are dotted with villages and market towns of great character and charm. It is ideal country for ramblers.

There is, too, much to be said in praise of the gem of a guidebook contained in the pages that follow. The reader will quickly appreciate the author's diligence, clarity and unbounded enthusiasm for his project.

As Bob Kirk points out in his Introduction, the Shropshire Way came into being through the efforts of Ramblers' Association groups and clubs working in collaboration with the county council. Bob himself is Secretary of the RA Midland Area and, in that capacity, has done much to strengthen the Association in the Midlands and to increase our membership. He has now produced a guidebook which will doubtless prove a great success with walkers—and deservedly so.

Therefore, dear reader, if you enjoy walking the Shropshire Way and find this guide to be an invaluable companion, do consider making a gesture of appreciation to the author and all the other voluntary workers from the Ramblers' Association who made your walk possible. Become a member yourself, so that the RA can continue to protect ancient paths and open up many more new routes like the glorious Shropshire Way.

Alan Mattingly
Secretary, The Ramblers' Association
September 1982

ACKNOWLEDGEMENTS

'....... in this book I have only made up a bunch of other people's flowers, and of my own I have only provided the string that ties them together.'

Montaigne

So in keeping with this sentiment I must sincerely thank fellow ramblers who have walked parts of the Shropshire Way with me, and who have also supplied information about the route and checked the details of my maps. In particular I am grateful to Eve Powell, Derek Pountney, Clem Rollason, Tim Wastling, Dr Bryan Willoughby, and Nick Wright of our various Ramblers' Association Groups in Shropshire. I must also thank Malcolm Hoskins of the Shrewsbury Rambling and Hillwalking Club and Bob Parry of Wem Walkers who have also given information about the sections of the route pioneered by their clubs.

Finally I must record special thanks to my wife Sheila, who has checked the manuscript and has been companion, chauffeur, and patient listener to hours of nonsensical talk about footpaths and public rights of way.

KEY TO MAP SYMBOLS

road-fenced

road-unfenced

railway

urban housing

THE ROUTE

across fields or open hill.

on unsurfaced tracks or green lanes.

on metalled roads.

FIELD BOUNDARIES

hedge   wire.   wooden fence.

s	stile	G	gate	wkt	wicket gate
+	church	■	building	▵	triangulation point
ᛰ	tree-deciduous	⚘	tree-coniferous		compass bearing
FP	footpath sign	FB	footbridge	P	Parking

stream   power line

SCALE

one mile

All strip maps are drawn with North at the top of the page.

INTRODUCTION

The Shropshire Way is a recreational footpath created by linking together existing public rights of way on footpaths, bridleways, and quiet lanes. The route was planned by Shropshire rambling clubs and local groups of the Ramblers' Association in consultation with Shropshire County Council.
The clubs involved in planning the route were:-

Broseley and Much Wenlock R.A. Group.
East Shropshire R.A. Group.
Shropshire Rambling and Hillwalking Club.
South Shropshire R.A. Group.
Wem Walkers.
Whitchurch Walkers.

The route was the result of two years of work by members of these clubs who have waymarked sections of it and have cleared obstructions. It was appropriate that the Way was completed in 1980 to mark the Ramblers' Associaton's Footpath Heritage Year.

I first got to know the Shropshire Way with the Broseley and Much Wenlock R.A. Group on a cold February day. A day spent on Wenlock Edge clearing a section of overgrown lane and erecting two stiles. Two years later the experience of walking the Way in all seasons has reinforced my love of the Shropshire landscape. The county offers delightful and varied walking and I hope that this guide does justice to its many attractions.

THE ROUTE

The Shropshire Way uses 172 miles of footpaths, bridleways, and quiet country lanes. The main section of the Way is a loop of 125 miles with its northern-most point at Wem and its southern end at Ludlow. At Wem a spur branches northwards for 11 miles to link with the Sandstone Trail at Grindley Brook near Whitchurch. The Sandstone Trail follows the undulating range of hills which runs northwards across central Cheshire to near Ellesmere Port. A further extension of roughly 35 miles leaves the main route at Bridges Youth Hostel and crosses the Stiperstones to Bishops Castle and goes on via a section of Offa's Dyke to Clun. From Clun this extension then returns eastwards passing near the Iron Age hill fort of Bury Ditches, to rejoin the main route on Hopesay Hill. This addition crosses fine open country and provides some of the best walking in Shropshire.

The landscape traversed by the Way has been shaped by a long and complex geological history. Indeed the succession of rocks and the varied landforms of south Shropshire have made it classic geological ground. The scenery ranges from the distinctive beauty of the south Shropshire hills and Wenlock Edge to the quiet, gently undulating plain in the north of the county.

The open moor and common land of the Long Mynd, Stiperstones, and the Clee Hills is becoming increasingly well known and favoured by walkers. This is scenery which has been determined by the dip and fold of the underlying rocks and by fault lines. It is also the countryside which provides the setting for Housman's poems and the novels of Mary Webb.

The lowland scenery of the Corve and Teme valleys and the north Shropshire plain also has its attractions. One of the most pleasing is provided by the architecture of the historic houses and picturesque villages. The limestone frequently used in the south of the county mellows to a subdued ochre which blends naturally into the landscape. Shropshire is noted for decorative half-timbering, sometimes combined with stone or brick which has resulted in some of the most attractive buildings seen anywhere in England. The quiet field paths through the lowland parts of the county hold many surprises and are well worth exploring.

Attractive too are the wooded slopes of the Severn Gorge at Ironbridge which have been designated a site of special scientific interest. The interest in the site arises from the diverse ecology which has developed partly from the devastation caused to the woodland by industrial activity in the gorge. Now the scars are largely healed and an amazing variety of trees and plants have recolonised the site.

The Severn Gorge is fast becoming a fashionable shrine for tourists wishing to view the relics of the 18th and early 19th century industrial activity. These are being preserved by the Ironbridge Gorge Museum

Trust on several sites. The Way crosses Abraham Darby's famous bridge and passes through the maze of steps and alleyways which were built as the town of Ironbridge developed with the growth of iron smelting in the 1830's.

The primary loop of the Shropshire Way links the towns of Shrewsbury, Craven Arms, Ludlow, Much Wenlock, Ironbridge and Wem. It is possible to start the walk at any of these places. The circular nature of the route also makes it easy to plan short rambles of up to ten miles which include sections of the Way. These may appeal to ramblers not wishing to walk the Way continuously.

Disclaimer

The entire Shropshire Way follows public rights of way and every care has been taken to ensure the accuracy of the maps and route descriptions. The Author and Publishers cannot accept responsibility for any misinterpretation by users.

FINDING THE WAY

The strip maps in this guide are intended to supplement the information given on Ordnance Survey Maps. Where field boundaries have been removed the new field pattern is shown on the strip maps but the old boundaries will be printed on some O.S. sheets.

There are well-trodden paths over the more popular hilly sections of the route and frequently the Way uses existing farm tracks or green lanes where route finding will present no difficulty. Sections of the route too have been clearly waymarked.

Route finding across enclosed farm land basically involves finding the gate or stile in the next hedge. This is easy where fields are small but the economics of modern farming has led to the creation of large fields where the opposite boundary can sometimes be nearly a half-mile away. To cope with this problem compass bearings are given on the strip maps where they will help to establish the correct line to the next stile or gate.

The growth of some Shropshire hedgerows in summer is prolific with the result that sometimes stiles and wicket gates can be obscured by new shoots. It may sometimes be difficult to see the stile or gate in the opposite boundary but this problem should lessen as the route gets more frequent use.

A final point concerning stiles is worth noting. Old Shropshire stiles were constructed with stone footsteps and wooden rails. Over the years many of the stone steps have either gone or become overgrown so that only the rails remain. No distinction has been made, on the strip maps, between stiles with stone or wooden steps and those where the step is missing.

ARABLE FIELDS

The strip maps do not distinguish those fields seeded with arable crops from those which are pasture. Clearly land usage can change from year to year. Where a field is put to arable use walkers are advised to keep strictly to the line of the path since this is the only legal right of way. If you are walking with a party it is sensible to keep in single file. Even at the height of summer arable fields can be crossed with minimal damage occurring to the crop. Generally it is easier to walk arable fields in April or May when growing crops are below knee height and easier still after mid-August when they have usually been combined.

In contrast to cereal crops a large field of rape can present an impenetrable barrier when fully grown. Although obstruction of a public right of way by such a crop is illegal, the more agreable course if rape is encountered is to avoid the field and use a road. fortunately few such fields are likely to be met on the route and the problem only exists during the months of July and August.

BULLS

The Wildlife and Countryside Act regrettably has presented walkers with the hazard of sometimes encountering bulls with herds of cows. To allay fears I should say that no bull on the Shropshire Way has yet greeted me with more than a derisory snort, either when walking alone or when leading a rambling party. Nevertheless walkers should exercise great caution whenever a bull is met.

WHAT TO TAKE AND WEAR

In summer months conditions most of the Shropshire Way can be comfortably walked in strong shoes. The single exception is the Stiperstones where some block scree and heather has to be crossed and the ankle protection afforded by boots may be welcomed by some walkers.

In winter when crossing ploughed fields you can expect wet clinging soil to double the weight of your footwear. A factor in favour, perhaps, of starting out in lightweight boots. An alternative worth considering is the humble wellie. Certainly only wellies can cope with the viscous slurry which develops in winter at field gates due to the passage of cattle over waterlogged clay.

To fend off the rain an outer shell of waterproofed nylon is a good choice. A hooded jacket and overtrousers makes a complete set and the lighter weight garments pack into a small space. Underneath, layers of cotton, wool, or thermal clothing can be built up in whatever combination suits you or the season.

Take a rucsac to carry spare clothing, food, and camera. Find space for a first aid kit to cope with accidental bites, blisters, cuts, and grazes. Take a compass to set your map and to remove some of the guesswork from routefinding.

FOLLOW THE COUNTRY CODE

Guard against all risks of fire.
Fasten all gates.
Keep dogs under proper control.
Keep to paths across farm land.
Leave no litter.
Safeguard water supplies.
Protect wildlife, wild plants, and trees.
Go carefully on country roads.
Respect the life of the countryside.

MAPS

The strip maps contained in the guide are sufficient to allow the walker to follow the route but those requiring details of the surrounding countryside could consult the following Ordnance Survey maps.

1:50 000 Landranger Series Sheet numbers 117, 126, 137, 138.

1:25 000 1st Series SJ 42, SJ 43, SJ 44, SJ 51, SJ 52, SJ 60, SJ 61, SO 28, SO 38, SO 47, SO 48, SO 57, SO 58, SO 68, SO 69.

1:25 000 Pathfinder Series SJ 41/51, SO 49/59, SO 29/39.

Northern extension :
GRINDLEY BROOK
to Wem.   12 miles.

...wing bridge over the
...lesmere Canal near
...ackoe Cottages.

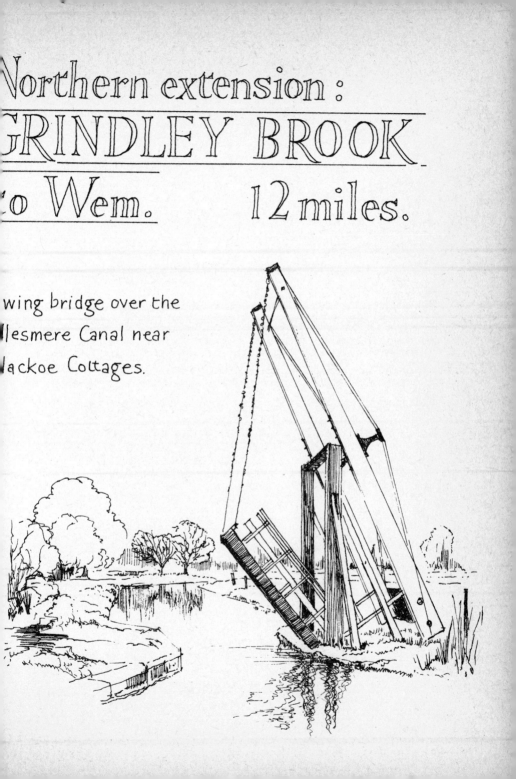

GRINDLEY BROOK to BLACKOE

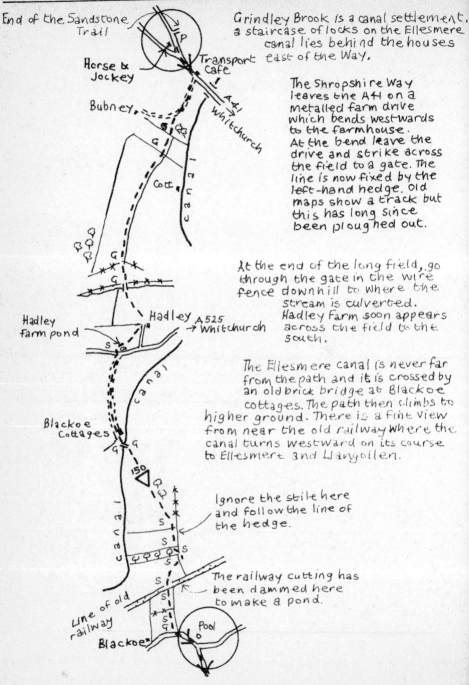

End of the Sandstone Trail

Horse & Jockey

Bubney

Transport Cafe

A41 Whitchurch

canal

Cott.

G

G

G

Hadley Farm pond

Hadley A525 → Whitchurch

canal

S G

Blackoe Cottages

G G

canal

150

S

S   S

S S

S

S

S
S
G

Line of old railway

Blackoe

Pool

Grindley Brook is a canal settlement, a staircase of locks on the Ellesmere canal lies behind the houses east of the Way.

The Shropshire Way leaves the A41 on a metalled farm drive which bends westwards to the farmhouse. At the bend leave the drive and strike across the field to a gate. The line is now fixed by the left-hand hedge. Old maps show a track but this has long since been ploughed out.

At the end of the long field, go through the gate in the wire fence downhill to where the stream is culverted. Hadley Farm soon appears across the field to the south.

The Ellesmere canal is never far from the path and it is crossed by an old brick bridge at Blackoe cottages. The path then climbs to higher ground. There is a fine view from near the old railway where the canal turns westward on its course to Ellesmere and Llangollen.

Ignore the stile here and follow the line of the hedge.

The railway cutting has been dammed here to make a pond.

16

The northern approach
to Hadley Farm.

Higher Bank near Whixall.

BLACKOE TO WHIXALL

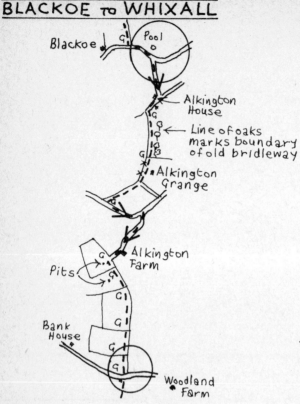

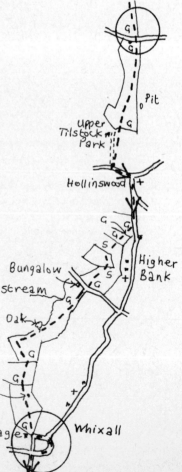

The lowland of North Shropshire has undergone several periods of glaciation. The old land surface was completely changed. Hollows in the pre-glacial landscape have been filled with deposits of clay or gravel. In other places lakes and meres occupy hollows created by the glacial drift.

A land surface of gravelly soils supports open heath and the wetter parts become fen covered with alder scrub or peat bog.

Whixall Moss was once such a landscape. Since Medieval times it has been enclosed and drained and today it is a landscape of small fields and scattered red brick farm houses. Small pools occupy hollows in the drift from which peat or gravel has been extracted.

WHIXALL to EDSTASTON.

The Way leaves Whixall by the road signposted 'Braynes Hall'. The lane leading directly to the signpost at the road junction is only passable in dry weather.

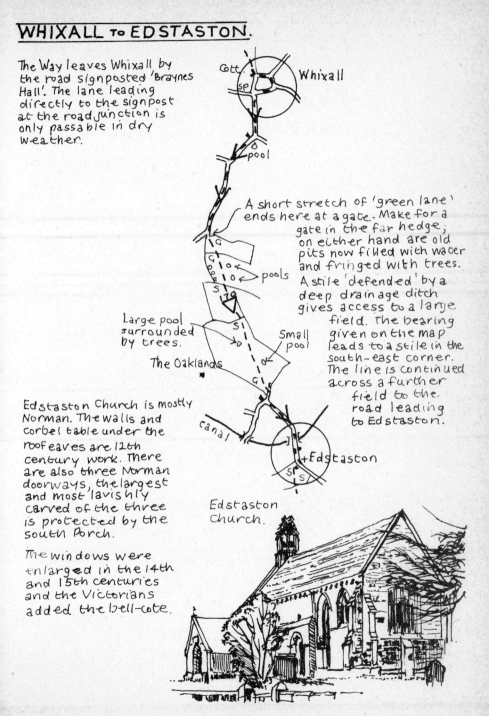

A short stretch of 'green lane' ends here at a gate. Make for a gate in the far hedge; on either hand are old pits now filled with water and fringed with trees. A stile 'defended' by a deep drainage ditch gives access to a large field. The bearing given on the map leads to a stile in the south-east corner. The line is continued across a further field to the road leading to Edstaston.

Large pool surrounded by trees.

The Oaklands

Small pool

Edstaston Church is mostly Norman. The walls and corbel table under the roof eaves are 12th century work. There are also three Norman doorways, the largest and most lavishly carved of the three is protected by the south porch.

The windows were enlarged in the 14th and 15th centuries and the Victorians added the bell-cote.

Edstaston Church.

19

EDSTASTON TO WEM.

Edstaston

pools

Whitchurch

B5476

Pools

Highfields

Cemetery

Drawwell Walk

WEM

railway

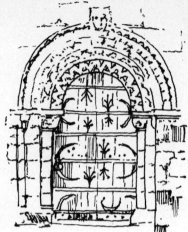

North Doorway, Edstaston Church
Norman Period.

The Way leaves Edstaston at a stile opposite the eastern end of the church. The footpath runs adjacent to the drive of a house to a second stile at the rear.

Now cross the large field to a stile in the wire fence passing between two tree fringed pools. The route goes south to a stile in the corner of the boundary fence. A succession of stiles then indicate the way across pasture to a gate opposite the lane leading to Highfields Farm.

Highfields stands on the site of a medieval farmstead. It is some way from the Norman settlement of Edstaston and it must have required some courage to colonise a lonely site away from the communal security of the village. Evidence of its isolation lies in the existence of a former moat which gave protection against wild animals and vagrants who were, presumably, quite unlike the peaceful ramblers who pass this way today.

A succession of stiles lead across small pastures to the modern housing estates on the outskirts of Wem. The best way to the centre of the town is via Drawwell Walk

Main route :
WEM to
SHREWSBURY. 15 miles.

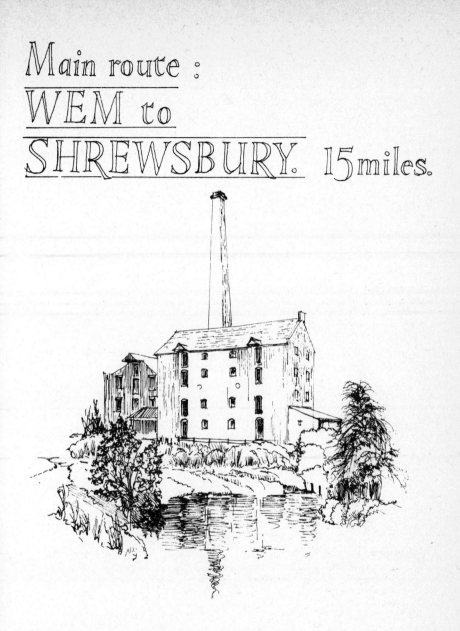

Mill on the River Roden, Wem.

WEM TO TILLEY GREEN

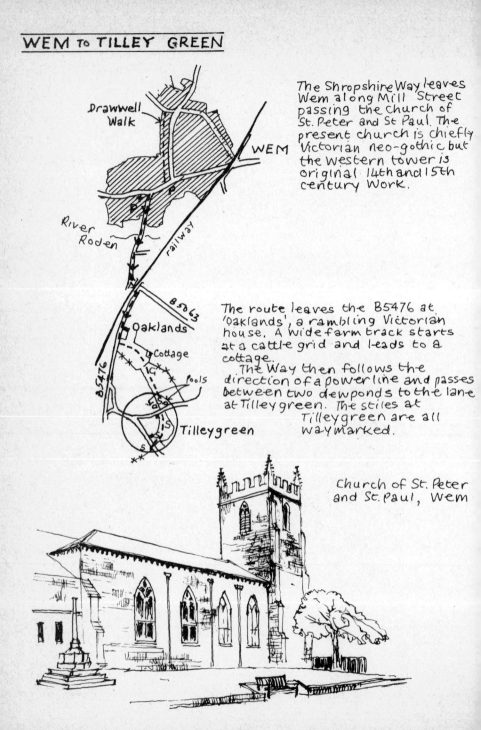

Drawwell Walk

WEM

The Shropshire Way leaves Wem along Mill Street passing the church of St. Peter and St Paul. The present church is chiefly Victorian neo-gothic but the western tower is original 14th and 15th century work.

River Roden

railway

B5063

Oaklands

Cottage

IG

Pools

B5476

Tilleygreen

The route leaves the B5476 at 'Oaklands', a rambling Victorian house. A wide farm track starts at a cattle grid and leads to a cottage.

The Way then follows the direction of a power line and passes between two dewponds to the lane at Tilleygreen. The stiles at Tilleygreen are all waymarked.

Church of St. Peter and St. Paul, Wem

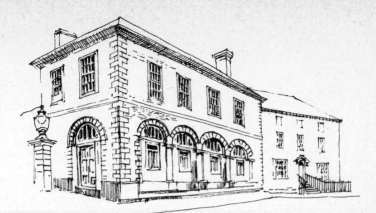

19th Century Market Hall, Wem.
The arches were formerly
open to the street.

The Mill is a clear
landmark on the road
out of Wem.

WEM MILLS LTD

Sandstone Crags under
the summit of Grinshill.

The spire of Clive Church
from Grinshill.

TILLEY GREEN TO GRINSHILL

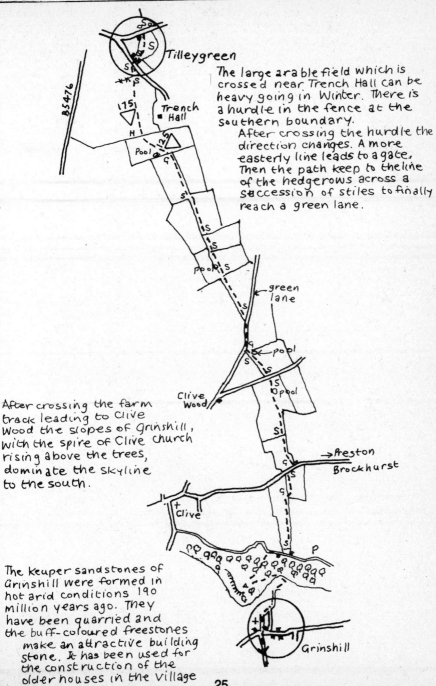

Tilleygreen

Trench Hall

Pool

The large arable field which is crossed near Trench Hall can be heavy going in Winter. There is a hurdle in the fence at the southern boundary.

After crossing the hurdle the direction changes. A more easterly line leads to a gate. Then the path keep to the line of the hedgerows across a succession of stiles to finally reach a green lane.

green lane

pool

Clive Wood

pool

After crossing the farm track leading to Clive Wood the slopes of Grinshill, with the spire of Clive church rising above the trees, dominate the skyline to the south.

Preston Brockhurst

Clive

The Keuper sandstones of Grinshill were formed in hot arid conditions 190 million years ago. They have been quarried and the buff-coloured freestones make an attractive building stone. It has been used for the construction of the older houses in the village

Grinshill

25

GRINSHILL TO ASTLEY

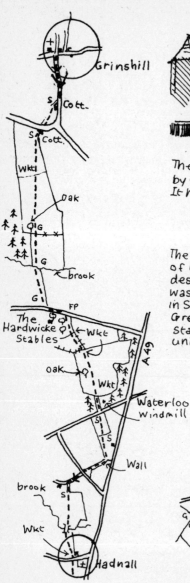

The Shropshire Way leaves Grinshill village by the lane opposite this fine stone house. It has a sundial mounted high on the wall.

The Hardwicke Stables are all that remain of Hardwicke Grange, a neo-gothic mansion designed by Thomas Harrison. Harrison was responsible for Lord Hill's column in Shrewsbury, said to be the tallest Greek Doric Column in the world. The stables have now been let as workshop units for rural craftsmen.

Hadnall

The detour which crosses the railway to Hadnall Wood Farm allows the walker to avoid using the busy A49.

Grinshill from the south.

Windmill built by Viscount Hill in memory
of his exploits at Waterloo.

ASTLEY to HAUGHMOND ABBEY.

The striking facade of Astley House will be seen when walking south on the lane leading from the village. The house is Georgian but is embellished with large Corinthian pilasters and an entrance porch supported by Doric columns.

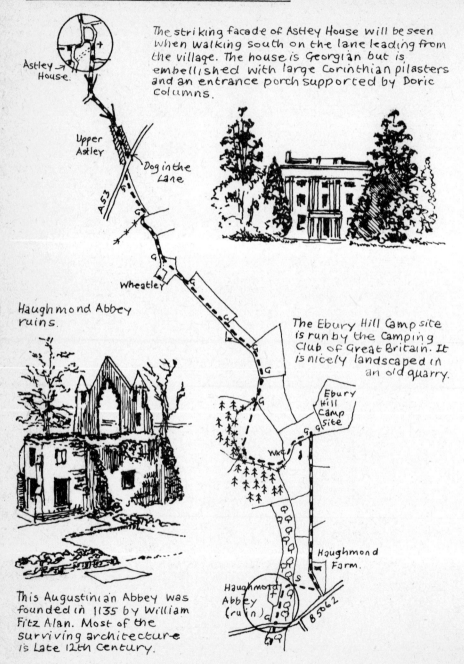

Astley House.

Upper Astley

A53

Dog in the Lane

Wheatley

Haughmond Abbey ruins.

The Ebury Hill Camp site is run by the Camping Club of Great Britain. It is nicely landscaped in an old quarry.

Ebury Hill Camp Site

Wkt

Haughmond Farm.

Haughmond Abbey (ruin)

B5062

This Augustinian Abbey was founded in 1135 by William Fitz Alan. Most of the surviving architecture is Late 12th Century.

HAUGHMOND ABBEY TO SHREWSBURY CASTLE

Haughmond Abbey was founded around 1135 but most of the remains above ground are of a later date. The abbey was built so close to Haughmond Hill that some walls have their foundations hewn out of solid rock.

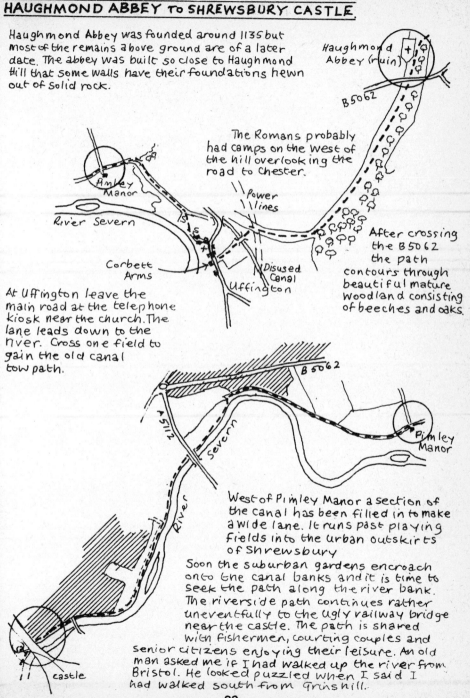

The Romans probably had camps on the west of the hill overlooking the road to Chester.

After crossing the B5062 the path contours through beautiful mature woodland consisting of beeches and oaks.

At Uffington leave the main road at the telephone kiosk near the church. The lane leads down to the river. Cross one field to gain the old canal tow path.

West of Pimley Manor a section of the canal has been filled in to make a wide lane. It runs past playing fields into the urban outskirts of Shrewsbury

Soon the suburban gardens encroach onto the canal banks and it is time to seek the path along the river bank. The riverside path continues rather uneventfully to the ugly railway bridge near the castle. The path is shared with fishermen, courting couples and senior citizens enjoying their leisure. An old man asked me if I had walked up the river from Bristol. He looked puzzled when I said I had walked south from Grinshill.

The English Bridge, Shrewsbury.

This bridge dates from 1768 and it replaced
a medieval structure with houses on.
Walkers aiming for the Youth Hostel
should leave the route at this point.

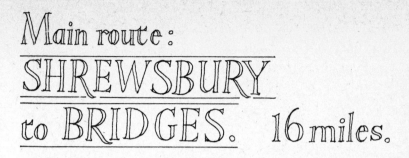

Main route:
SHREWSBURY
to BRIDGES. 16 miles.

Kingsland Bridge, Shrewsbury.

SHREWSBURY CASTLE to LYTHWOOD FARM.

The river is crossed at Kingsland Bridge.
This is a Victorian suspension bridge
using an iron arch with a span of 212 feet.

The outskirts of Shrewsbury are reached
surprisingly quickly which is a pity
because there is much to see in this
fine old historic city. Travellers
walking the Way continuously
could use a 'rest' day for a sight-
seeing perambulation of the city.

'The Castle' at Bayston Hill.

The castle' is a tall white
house which dominates the
skyline beyond a large
field south-west of Pulley.
The path passes alongside
t into Castle Lane.

The Longmyndian series
of Pre-Cambrian rocks lie
beneath the housing
estate on Bayston Hill.
They are some of the oldest
rocks to be found in England
and Wales. They were laid down
as sediments in shallow water.

LYTHWOOD FARM to THE VINNALS

The route south from Lythwood Farm follows a wide tractor track across a largely treeless prairie of large arable fields bounded by wire fences. Modern farming methods do not create varied or picturesque countryside and fortunately the arable fields end at the low tree-covered ridge of Lyth Hill.

Lyth Hill is a good viewpoint, the ground falls steeply away to the south and there is an uninterrupted view to the shapely group of hills around Church Stretton.

There are houses and a Windmill on the northern slopes of Lyth Hill. Note the gate leading to Spring Cottage. This was the home of the novelist Mary Webb from 1917 until she died in 1927.

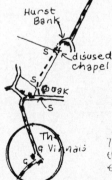

The path leads off the hill through patches of gorse with a scattering of bluebells and stitchwort.

An unsurfaced lane leads from Exfords Green to end at Hurst Bank farm. Behind the farmhouse is a disused primitive methodist chapel dated 1831. It is now a store for farm implements.

The drive to 'The Vinnals' carries the farm's name on a sign at the entrance.

THE VINNALS TO WILDERLEY HALL

The Way continues through the farmyard and along a wide unsurfaced track bordered by hedgerows. The track fords a stream and the crossing may be difficult in wet weather.

Beyond the ford is a barrier where the track narrows and becomes overgrown. It is easily passable for a further 440 yards to where a ditch flows across the lane. The going remains very wet until the last field's length to the drive to Castle Place.

The footbridge here is broken but the stream is usually easy to cross. If in doubt use the lane.

At Upper Moat Cottage the easiest way to the lane is to cross the ford in the farmyard. This is a diversion from the right of way which is badly obstructed.

The Vinnals

Ford

barrier

Castle Place

The Gorse

S
S
S
FB
S
G

Upper Moat Cottage

There follows 1½ miles of lane to Wilderley Hall. Lane walking would be dull but for the cry of the curlew and the plants in the hedgerows. Here are to be found, bluebell, germander speedwell, stitchwort, primrose, purple vetch, violets..... If I were more knowledgeable I could list more.

Wilderley Hall

Wilderley Lane Farm

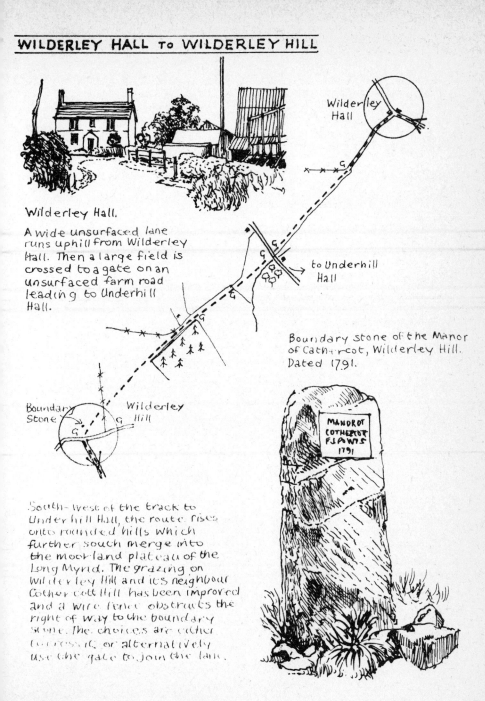

Wilderley Hall.

A wide unsurfaced lane runs uphill from Wilderley Hall. Then a large field is crossed to a gate on an unsurfaced farm road leading to Underhill Hall.

Boundary stone of the Manor of Cothercot, Wilderley Hill. Dated 1791.

South-West of the track to Underhill Hall, the route rises onto rounded hills which further south merge into the moorland plateau of the Long Mynd. The grazing on Wilderley Hill and its neighbour Cother cott Hill has been improved and a wire fence obstructs the right of way to the boundary stone. The choices are either to cross it, or alternatively use the gate to join the lane.

WILDERLEY HILL to BRIDGES
LOW LEVEL ROUTE

At Wilderley Hill there is a choice of route to Bridges. The more direct low level route takes the valley of the Darnford Brook to Ratlinghope. The path continues through woodland to Bridges.

The lane leading south from near the boundary stone at first has a metalled surface. This ends at a gate ¼ mile north-west of Betchcott Hill. The path to Lower Darnford descends into Golden Valley. This name is given on the O.S. map and may derive from the patches of gorse which years ago could have been more widespread than they are today.

Ratlinghope has been identified as the village of 'Slepe' in Mary Webb's novels. The village was associated with a real adventure which can match any fiction. The Rev. Donald Carr set out from the church during a January afternoon in 1865 aiming to reach Woolstaston. He became lost in the snow and staggered down into Cardingmill Valley twenty-seven hours later.

The Stiperstones seen beyond Golden Valley.

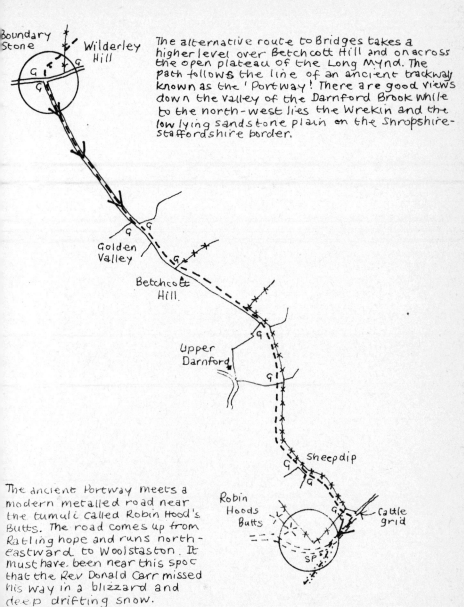

The alternative route to Bridges takes a higher level over Betchcott Hill and on across the open plateau of the Long Mynd. The path follows the line of an ancient trackway known as the 'Portway'. There are good views down the valley of the Darnford Brook while to the north-west lies the Wrekin and the low lying sandstone plain on the Shropshire-Staffordshire border.

Boundary Stone

Wilderley Hill

Golden Valley

Betchcott Hill.

Upper Darnford

Sheepdip

Robin Hoods Butts

Cattle grid

The ancient Portway meets a modern metalled road near the tumuli called Robin Hood's Butts. The road comes up from Ratlinghope and runs north-eastward to Woolstaston. It must have been near this spot that the Rev Donald Carr missed his way in a blizzard and deep drifting snow.

Corndon Hill from near Priory Cottage.

Looking south along the Long Mynd
boundary fault.

ROBIN HOODS BUTTS TO BRIDGES

The Way now crosses the open moorland plateau of the Long Mynd. A signpost indicates the direction of the Shooting Box near the Burway. The Burway is the metalled road which crosses the Long Mynd from Church Stretton to Ratlinghope. A path leads directly from the Burway to the triangulation point on Pole Bank.

The route to Bridges leaves the Burway west of the path to Pole Bank. An easy graded wide grassy track gives delightful walking.

The Stiperstones and Corndon Hill dominate the western skyline on the descent to Priory Cottage.

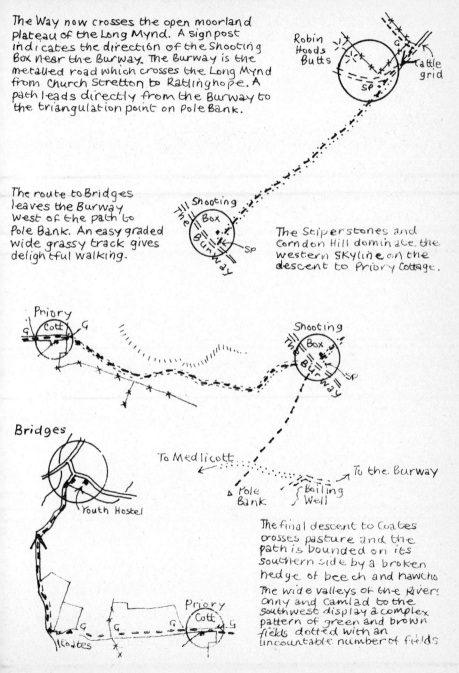

The final descent to Coates crosses pasture and the path is bounded on its southern side by a broken hedge of beech and hawtho

The wide valleys of the Rivers Onny and Camlad to the southwest display a complex pattern of green and brown fields dotted with an uncountable number of fields

The Clee Hills from
the Long Mynd.

Clun extension:
BRIDGES to CLUN
to HOPESAY HILL.
35 miles.

The Youth Hostel,
Clun.

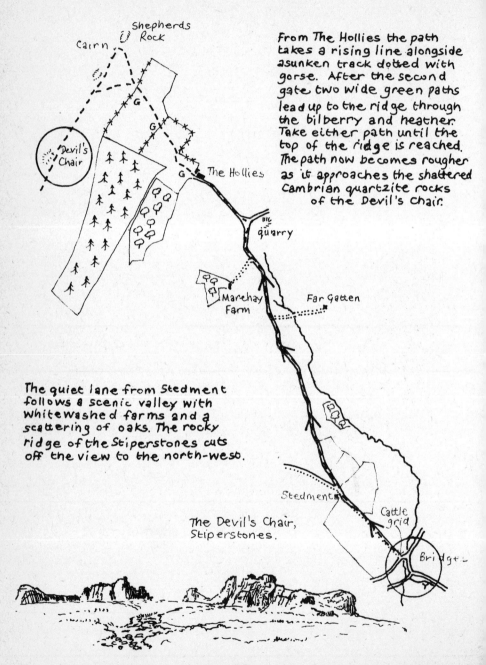

Cairn

Shepherds Rock

Devil's Chair

The Hollies

quarry

Marehay Farm

Far Gatten

Stedment

Cattle grid

Bridges

From The Hollies the path takes a rising line alongside a sunken track dotted with gorse. After the second gate two wide green paths lead up to the ridge through the bilberry and heather. Take either path until the top of the ridge is reached. The path now becomes rougher as it approaches the shattered Cambrian quartzite rocks of the Devil's chair.

The quiet lane from Stedment follows a scenic valley with whitewashed farms and a scattering of oaks. The rocky ridge of the Stiperstones cuts off the view to the north-west.

The Devil's Chair, Stiperstones.

DEVIL'S CHAIR TO RIDGE FARM.

The Stiperstones provide the best walking on the Shropshire Way. The path is well-worn, and rough. The triangulation point on Manstone Rock can be reached by a variety of scrambles. Descend by a sloping slab to the south-west and cross the scree to rejoin the main path.

Near Cranberry Rock a path leaves the ridge to join the road at a car park. The route follows a path on the western side of the rock which overlooks the woods at Nipstone Rock and meets the road at a gate.

After leaving the plantation a rough track leads through the heather to the prominent rock. The descent to Rock House needs care. The direct descent to the ruined house crosses steep scree while the path westward crosses a short stretch of block scree overgrown with heather. After Rock House a track leads down to the road at a gate. Descend the field opposite, cross the stream and wire fence, then a very steep climb to rejoin the lane.

The path crosses the stile here and follows the fence inside the plantation to join a ride through the next woodland section. I dislike walking through conifer plantations. The view is lost and rides have a nasty habit of leading in the wrong direction. This one fortunately is straight. After a half mile there is the compensation of a fine open view to Corndon Hill.

The Beech Avenue, Linley Hill.

Linley Hall.

RIDGE FARM TO LYDHAM

At the second gate on left past Ridge Farm, climb uphill across pasture keeping near the fence. The best views are behind you! Continue through the gate alongside the fence and soon the line of beeches on Linley Hill come into view.

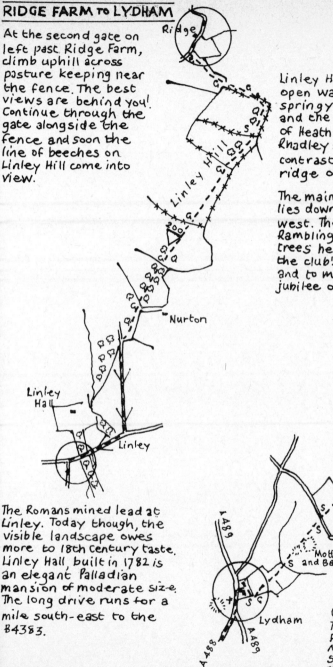

Linley Hill gives fine open walking on short springy turf. The beeches and the rounded shapes of Heath Mynd and Black Rhadley are in marked contrast to the rocky ridge of the Stiperstones.

The main avenue of beeches lies downhill to the south-west. The Birmingham CKA Rambling Club planted trees here to commemorate the club's 75th anniversary and to mark the silver jubilee of Queen Elizabeth II.

The Romans mined lead at Linley. Today though, the visible landscape owes more to 18th century taste. Linley Hall, built in 1782 is an elegant Palladian mansion of moderate size. The long drive runs for a mile south-east to the B4385.

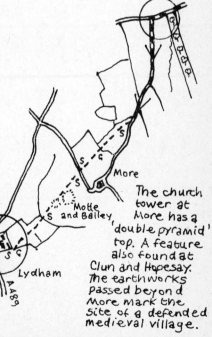

The church tower at More has a 'double-pyramid' top. A feature also found at Clun and Hopesay. The earthworks passed beyond More mark the site of a defended medieval village.

LYDHAM To BISHOPS CASTLE.

The village of More was probably
created after the Norman Conquest
with a castle at the western end
and the church at the east. The
layout at *Lydham* is similar with a
motte and bailey site placed west
of the church.

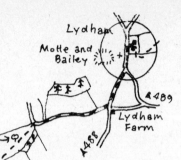

The bridleway which
leaves the A488 at
Lydham Farm turns
sharply north by a
strip of woodland. At
the bend are three
gates. Take the middle,
double gate, pass to
the south of a solitary
oak and find the gate
in the south-west
corner. Cross into the
next field and follow
the hedge to a gate
overlooking Upper
Heblands. Walk to
the main road via the
farm drive.

Bishops Castle

BISHOPS CASTLE TO REILTH TOP

The stream at Dogkennel Lane is now culverted but the footbridge at the former ford still remains in position.

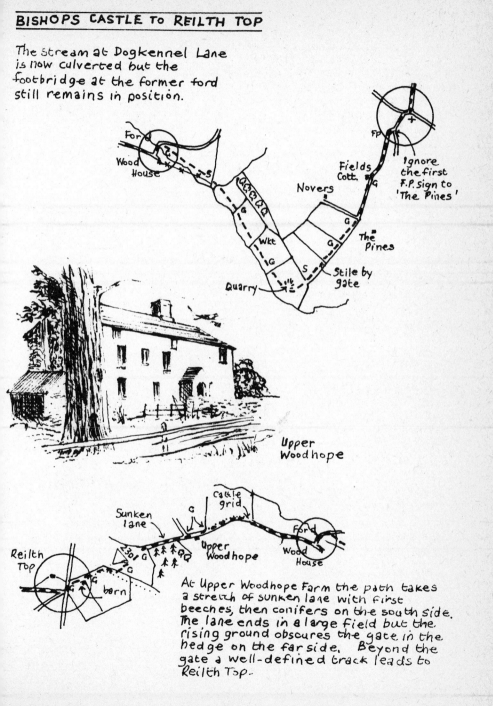

Upper Woodhope

At Upper Woodhope Farm the path takes a stretch of sunken lane with first beeches, then conifers on the south side. The lane ends in a large field but the rising ground obscures the gate in the hedge on the far side. Beyond the gate a well-defined track leads to Reilth Top.

REILTH TOP TO THREE GATES.

Take the right hand track from the lane at Reilth Top to the ruined farm of Fron. Many of the pines in the windbreak have now fallen. The fenced path now descends to Reilth with good views down the Unk Valley.

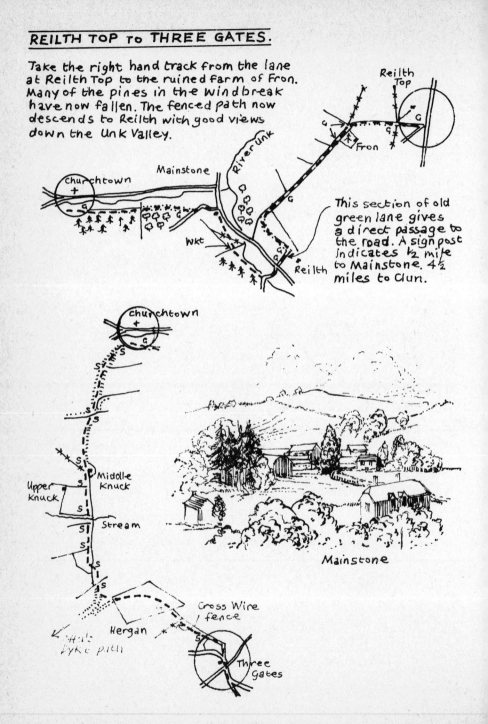

This section of old green lane gives a direct passage to the road. A signpost indicates ½ mile to Mainstone. 4½ miles to Clun.

Mainstone

THREE GATES TO CLUN

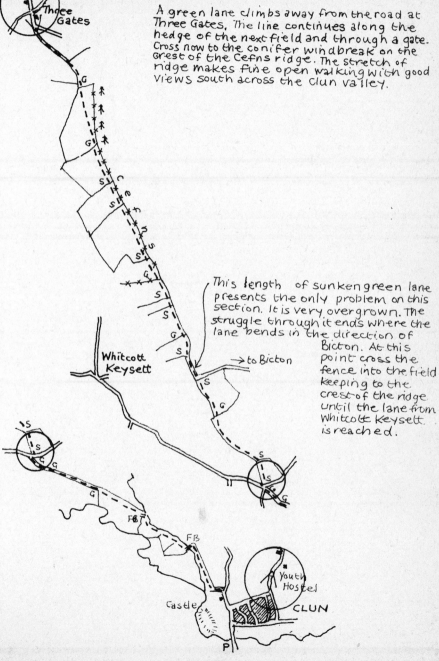

A green lane climbs away from the road at Three Gates. The line continues along the hedge of the next field and through a gate. Cross now to the conifer windbreak on the crest of the Cefns ridge. The stretch of ridge makes fine open walking with good views south across the Clun valley.

This length of sunken green lane presents the only problem on this section. It is very overgrown. The struggle through it ends where the lane bends in the direction of Bicton. At this point cross the fence into the field keeping to the crest of the ridge until the lane from Whitcott Keysett is reached.

Three Gates

G

G

S

Cefns

S

S

G

S

S

G

S

Whitcott Keysett

→ to Bicton

S

G

S

S

S

G

S

G

G

FB

FB

Youth Hostel

Castle

CLUN

P

49

CLUN TO BURY DITCHES

Bury Ditches is one of the most formidable Iron Age forts in South Shropshire. The fort dates from the 1st century B.C. It had two entrances, that on the N.E. side is protected by five banks. The north and west sides are defended by four banks and ditches. The people who lived in these Shropshire hill forts had no pottery or metal equipment which has survived. Their utensils must have been of wood or skin. The forts in this area were abandoned for reasons which still baffle archeologists.

Anyone sharing my aversion to being confined within lines of conifers will welcome the view north across the Kemp valley from the highest point on the track. The village below is Brockton and the farm with the tall silo to the north-west is at Acton.

Leave the extraction road where it swings round the head of the valley coming up from Clunton. and take the grassy ride leading steadily uphill.

The lane enters a section of coppiced oaks and joins a surfaced extraction road near an old quarry.

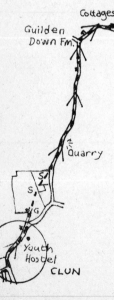

Quarry

Bury Ditches

firebreaks

Quarry

Cottages

Guilden Down Fm.

Quarry

Youth Hostel

CLUN

Near the hostel gate a footpath leaves the lane at the left side of a wooden garage. It crosses two fields and rejoins the lane to Guilden Down saving a half mile of tarmac. There is however, no way of avoiding the lane to reach Guilden Down and the cottages beyond, so relax and become a better botanist. Stitchwort, buttercup, purple vetch, germander speedwell, red campion, and wild parsley are some of the more common plants to catch the eye in May or June.

Beyond the cottages the track is unmetalled and finally becomes a rutted green lane as it enters the wood. Conifers have been planted beyond the immediate lane boundary of chestnut, oak, and ash.

URY DITCHES TO HOPESAY

Lower Down
G
G
G
Quarry
Stanley Cott.
At Stanley Cottage cross to the footpath on the south bank of the stream.
Walcot Lodge
ury Ditches

Walcot Lodge
Quarry
Cattle grid
Cott
FB
G
Kempton
Leave the estate road at the group of mature lime trees and cross the pasture to the white cottage

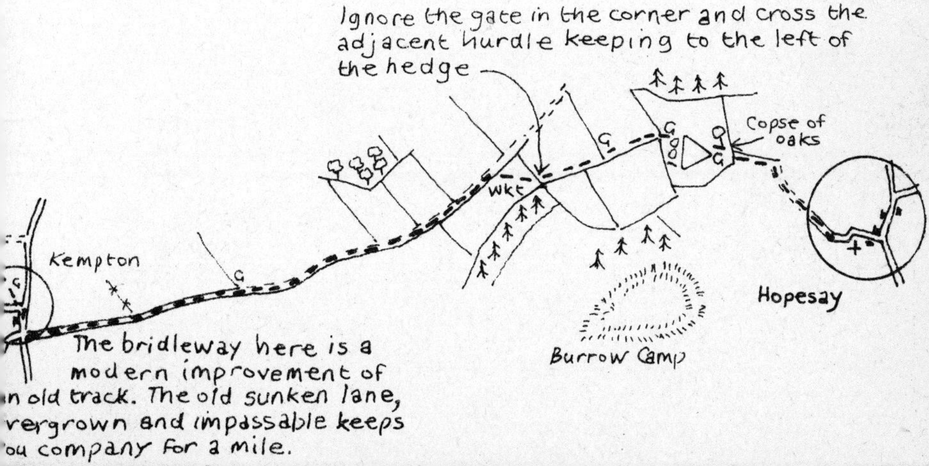

Ignore the gate in the corner and cross the adjacent hurdle keeping to the left of the hedge
G
G
Copse of oaks
G
Wkt
G
Kempton
Hopesay
Burrow Camp
The bridleway here is a modern improvement of an old track. The old sunken lane, overgrown and impassable keeps you company for a mile.

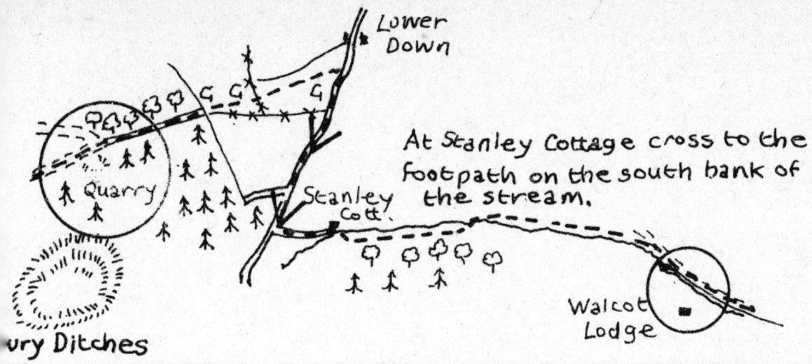

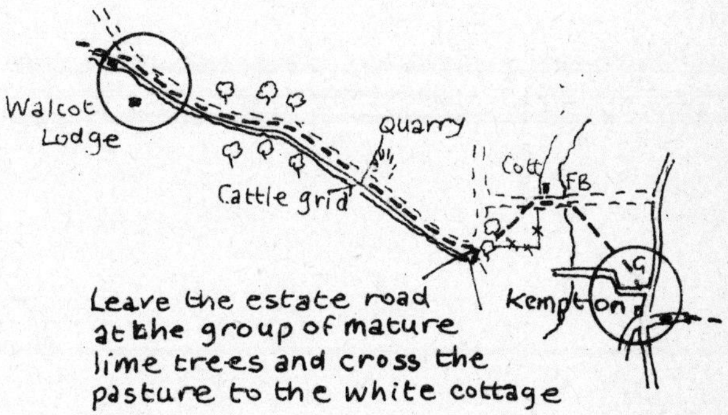

HOPESAY TO HOPESAY HILL

The Way leaves Hopesay on the minor road signposted Round Oak. The lane passing Brookside Cottage ends at a gate which gives access to Hopesay Common. A fairly direct line can be struck through the bracken to a small stand of conifers. Here the ground levels and a broad grassy path runs east to rejoin the main route.

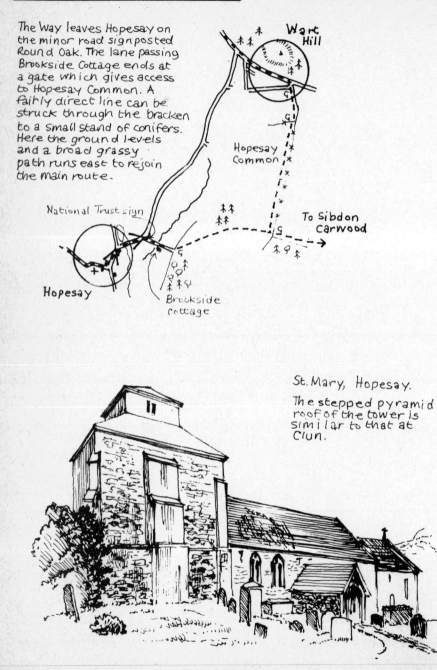

Wart Hill

Hopesay Common

National Trust sign

To Sibdon Carwood →

Hopesay

Brookside cottage

St. Mary, Hopesay.

The stepped pyramid roof of the tower is similar to that at Clun.

Main route:
BRIDGES to LUDLOW.
22 miles.

The hamlet of Bridges from the
slopes of Aasrone Hill.

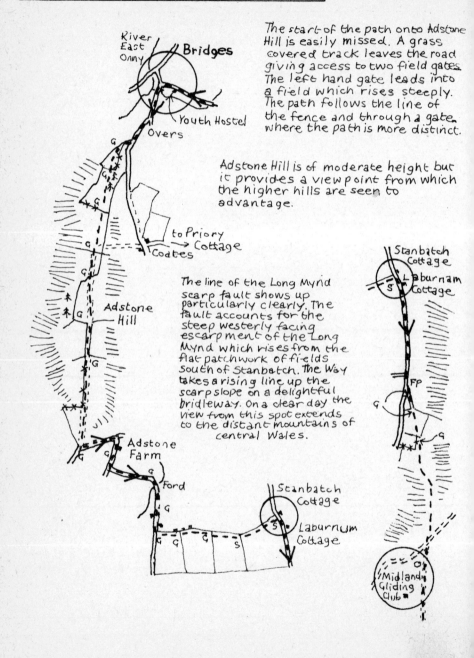

The start of the path onto Adstone Hill is easily missed. A grass covered track leaves the road giving access to two field gates. The left hand gate leads into a field which rises steeply. The path follows the line of the fence and through a gate where the path is more distinct.

Adstone Hill is of moderate height but it provides a viewpoint from which the higher hills are seen to advantage.

The line of the Long Mynd scarp fault shows up particularly clearly. The fault accounts for the steep westerly facing escarpment of the Long Mynd which rises from the flat patchwork of fields south of Stanbatch. The Way takes a rising line up the scarp slope on a delightful bridleway. On a clear day the view from this spot extends to the distant mountains of central Wales.

The Stiperstones from
Adstone Hill.

Adstone Farm.

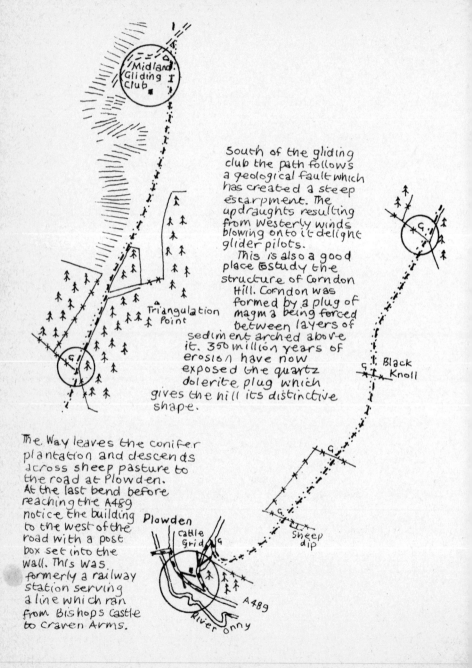

South of the gliding club the path follows a geological fault which has created a steep escarpment. The updraughts resulting from westerly winds blowing onto it delight glider pilots.

This is also a good place to study the structure of Corndon Hill. Corndon was formed by a plug of magma being forced between layers of sediment arched above it. 350 million years of erosion have now exposed the quartz dolerite plug which gives the hill its distinctive shape.

The Way leaves the conifer plantation and descends across sheep pasture to the road at Plowden. At the last bend before reaching the A489 notice the building to the west of the road with a post box set into the wall. This was formerly a railway station serving a line which ran from Bishops Castle to Craven Arms.

Midland Gliding Club

Triangulation Point

Black Knoll

Plowden

cattle Grid

sheep dip

A489

River Onny

PLOWDEN to WART HILL

A minor road leading to Edgton leaves the A489 and crosses the River Onny. The Way leaves the road along a private drive signposted as a public bridleway. A second sign points into the wood to where three tracks diverge. The centre track is the correct line.

The channel through which the River Onny flows eastwards to Craven Arms, was cut by the melt waters of a glacier lying to the north west. The steep sides are evidence that the channel is a geologically recent feature.

The path turns eastwards and makes a rising traverse through the conifers growing on the south side of the channel. At the top of the climb a wicket gate leads out into pastures which descend gently to Edgton.

Opposite the village hall a bridleway leads downhill to join a farm track. The track is left at a sharp bend and the Way climbs steeply up along the line of a hedge. Two fields are crossed on rising ground followed by a descent across a third field to the lane leading through the scattered hamlet of Round Oak to the foot of Wart Hill.

Plowden

Fp

A489

River Onny

FP

Wkt

Village Hall

Edgton

Telephone Kiosk

Round Oak

Wart Hill

Burrow Camp from near Round Oak.

WART HILL TO STOKESAY CASTLE

Wart Hill is something of a geological curiosity:- an island of ancient pre-Cambrian rock bounded on the east by Ordovician rocks and on the west by Silurian strata formed millions of years later. Wart Hill has a scattering of pine trees on its summit and it makes a good viewpoint.

The inlier of Cambrian rocks extends southwards onto Hopesay Common. Where the Way meets a path coming up from Hopesay village before turning eastwards.

Hopesay Common provides the last opportunity to enjoy the scenery of the Clun Forest at close hand

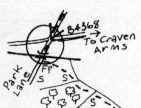

Wart Hill

Hopesay Common

To Hopesay village and route to Clun.

Cottage   Sibdon + Carwood

kissing gate

B4368

B4368 → To Craven Arms

Park Lane

Paddock

Stream

Stokesay Castle

A49 → To Ludlow

On leaving the wood Stokesay Castle and Church are seen below the wooded slopes of Norton Camp, an Iron Age hill fort. To the South the ground rises to View Edge which fully lives up to its name. Remember to return to explore it on your next walk.

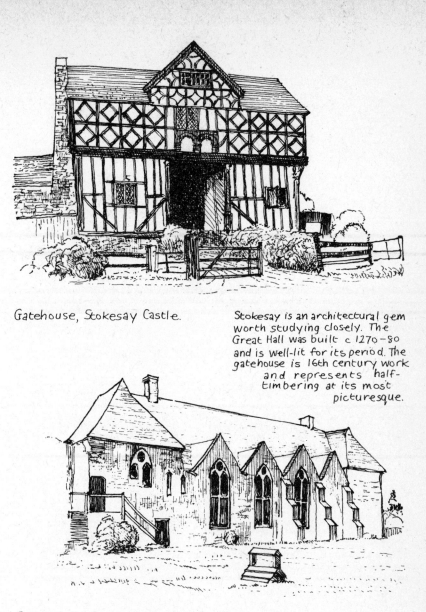

Gatehouse, Stokesay Castle.

Stokesay is an architectural gem worth studying closely. The Great Hall was built c 1270-80 and is well-lit for its period. The gatehouse is 16th century work and represents half-timbering at its most picturesque.

Great Hall, Stokesay Castle.

STOKESAY CASTLE to ONIBURY

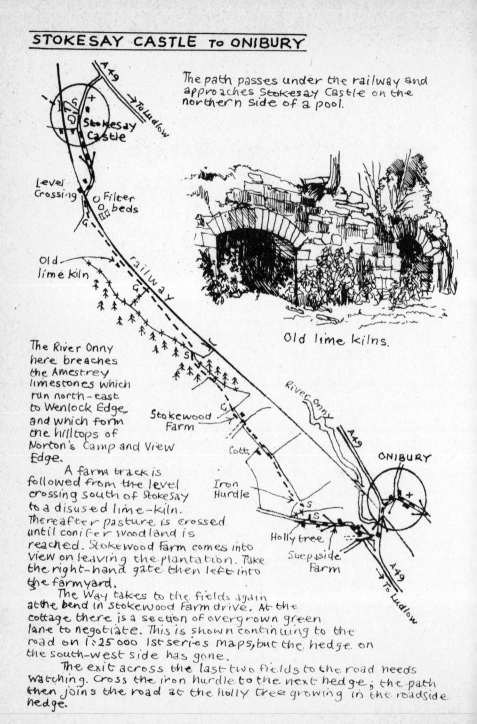

The path passes under the railway and approaches Stokesay Castle on the northern side of a pool.

A49
To Ludlow

Stokesay Castle

Level Crossing

o Filter o beds

Old lime kiln

railway

Old lime kilns.

The River Onny here breaches the Amestrey limestones which run north-east to Wenlock Edge and which form the hilltops of Norton's Camp and View Edge.

Stokewood Farm

River Onny

A49

ONIBURY

Cott.

A farm track is followed from the level crossing south of Stokesay to a disused lime-kiln. Thereafter pasture is crossed until conifer woodland is reached. Stokewood Farm comes into view on leaving the plantation. Take the right-hand gate then left into the farmyard.

Iron Hurdle

Holly tree

Steepside Farm

A49
To Ludlow

The Way takes to the fields again at the bend in Stokewood Farm drive. At the cottage there is a section of overgrown green lane to negotiate. This is shown continuing to the road on 1:25 000 1st series maps, but the hedge on the south-west side has gone.

The exit across the last two fields to the road needs watching. Cross the iron hurdle to the next hedge; the path then joins the road at the holly tree growing in the roadside hedge.

ONIBURY TO LUDLOW RACE COURSE

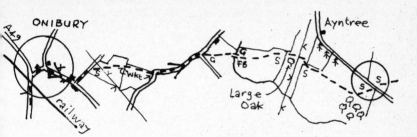

Leave Onibury by the unsurfaced lane near 'The Holly Bush. A stile leads into a pasture crossed by a power line. Wicket gates confirm the line alongside the hedge to the road.

The stile in the hedge west of the large oak is 'defended' by a ~~deep~~ muddy ditch. The summer growth in the hedgerows hereabouts is formidable. Some searching may have to be undertaken to find the stiles east of the oak until the drive to Poole Farm is reached

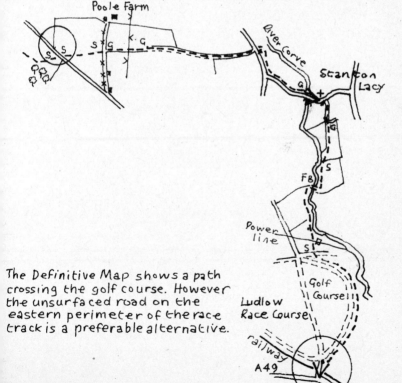

The Definitive Map shows a path crossing the golf course. However the unsurfaced road on the eastern perimeter of the race track is a preferable alternative.

Cruciform church of St. Peter, Stanton Lacy.

Two views on the approach to Ludlow.

LUDLOW RACE COURSE to LUDLOW

The church and the castle feature prominently in the skyline seen on the approach to Ludlow. They serve as reminders that the town was planted by the Normans. The castle became one of the most powerful fortresses in the Marches. The church is no less impressive with a tall central tower which is 135 ft. high. A memorial stone to the poet A. E. Houseman stands near the north door.

The Way enters the town by a quiet back street which ends on the site of Linney Gate on the line of the old Medieval town wall.

KEY TO HISTORIC BUILDINGS

1. Feathers Hotel.
2. Butter Cross.
3. Church of St. Laurence and Reader's House.
4. Angel Hotel.
5. Broad Gate.
6. Ludford Bridge.

This list might be compared to an aperitif for Ludlow provides an architectural feast which must not be bolted down.

The contrast between the narrow medieval streets and the more spaciously planned Georgian buildings in Broad Street creates the varied character which makes Ludlow one of the most pleasant of the Shropshire towns.

The Butter Cross, Ludlow.
A building in renaissance style
dating from 1743.

Main route :
LUDLOW to
IRONBRIDGE.   34 miles.

Titterstone Clee.

Broad Street, Ludlow.

Ludford Bridge.

HOPESCROSS to PILGRIM'S COTTAGE

Wilderhope Manor is the finest of the old houses situated along Wenlock Edge. It was built about 1535. Standing on its own, and sheltered by wooded hills at the head of a south facing valley, its appearance can have changed little in the past 400 years.

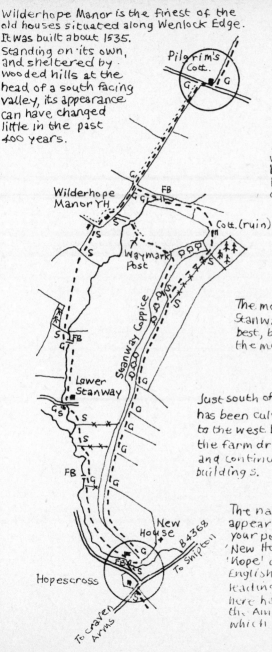

As an alternative to the valley route a path goes behind the cottages at Hopescross onto the crest of the escarpment. Though steeper, this path has the advantage of fine open views across the Corve to Brown Clee and down the valley to its confluence with the Teme

The more direct path down through Stanway Coppice to Wilderhope is best, but come again and explore the more northerly path.

Just south of Lower Stanway the stream has been culverted to provide a crossing to the west bank. The route then takes the farm drive back across the stream and continues between the farm buildings.

The name Hopescross does not appear on Landranger Maps but your position can be checked from 'New House' which is given. A 'Hope' derived from the old English word 'hop' is a side valley leading off a main one. The hope here has been cut along a joint in the Aymestry limestone by a stream which rises near Wilderhope.

St. Paul, Knowbury

Old quarry,
Titterstone Clee.

View to South-west, Titterstone Clee.

KNOWBURY CHURCH TO TITTERSTONE CLEE

The shapely mass of Titterstone Clee makes a striking feature in the beautiful landscape around Ludlow. Closer acquaintance reveals that Titterstone is scarred and desecrated by mineral extraction. Coal, iron basalt, and copper have been worked here since 1235. The long history of quarrying on the south side of Titterstone encouraged squatter settlement. By the 18th century a distinctive landscape of small fields and cottages had evolved which has remained to the present day.

Footbridge across Bensons Brook

The path climbs out of the valley cut by Benson's Brook and links with an old quarry road. The most direct route crosses the rough ground to the old mineral incline, and up it to the disused quarry. The summit can then be reached either by climbing round the western rim of the quarry or by walking along the road which serves the aerial installation.

The path here crosses a series of stiles in the boundaries of fields too small to be mapped on this scale. Two features confirm the line for you, the barn, which is falling down, and the stream crossing. The general direction is North-easterly.

TITTERSTONE CLEE TO WHEATHILL

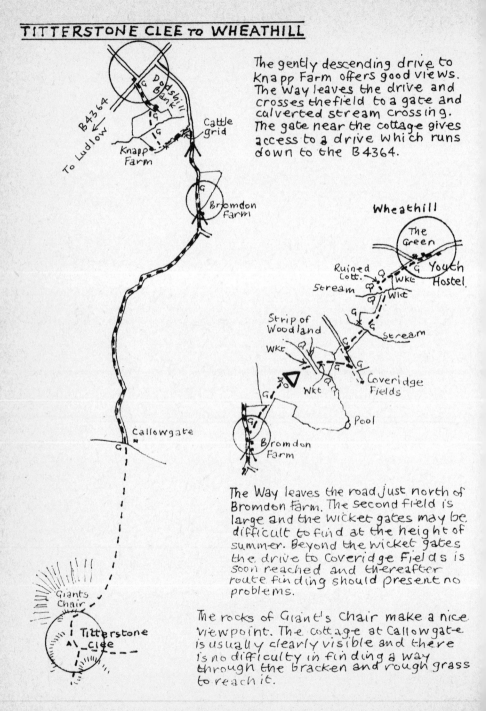

The gently descending drive to Knapp Farm offers good views. The Way leaves the drive and crosses the field to a gate and culverted stream crossing. The gate near the cottage gives access to a drive which runs down to the B4364.

The Way leaves the road just north of Bromdon Farm. The second field is large and the wicket gates may be difficult to find at the height of summer. Beyond the wicket gates the drive to Coveridge Fields is soon reached and thereafter route finding should present no problems.

The rocks of Giant's Chair make a nice viewpoint. The cottage at Callowgate is usually clearly visible and there is no difficulty in finding a way through the bracken and rough grass to reach it.

Radar installation, Titterstone Clee.

Brown Clee from
Giant's Chair.

Wheathill Youth Hostel

WHEATHILL TO BROWN CLEE

Nordybank is the best preserved of the Iron Age hill forts on Brown Clee. Surrounded by a single ditch, it probably served as a look-out post for the larger forts which occupied the summits of Abdon and Clee Burf.

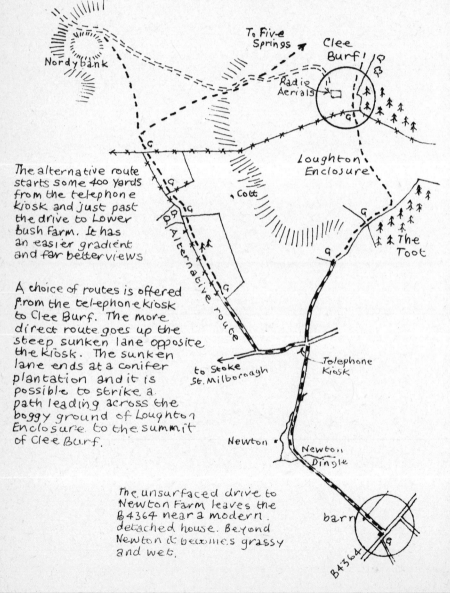

The alternative route starts some 400 yards from the telephone kiosk and just past the drive to Lower Bush Farm. It has an easier gradient and far better views

A choice of routes is offered from the telephone kiosk to Clee Burf. The more direct route goes up the steep sunken lane opposite the kiosk. The sunken lane ends at a conifer plantation and it is possible to strike a path leading across the boggy ground of Loughton Enclosure to the summit of Clee Burf.

The unsurfaced drive to Newton Farm leaves the B4364 near a modern detached house. Beyond Newton it becomes grassy and wet.

Abdon Burf.

Memorial tablet in memory of
the twenty-three allied and
German airmen who died in
flying accidents on Brown
Clee 1939-1945.

Nordybank.

CLEE BURF to UPPER EARNSTREY FARM.

Upper Earnstrey Farm.

Abdon Burf (1790 ft) is the highest point in Shropshire and the views, in all directions are extensive.

To Abdon

To Ditton Priors

Telephone Kiosk

Pool

Aerial Installation

Abdon Burf

Pool

The two tops of the Brown Clee have been scarred by quarrying but this ceased in 1936. The path from Clee Burf crosses coal measures which have been mined since medieval times. The circular depressions are old 'bell pits' This method of extracting coal continued here until the 17th century.

Memorial Stone

A small memorial stone has been placed in the heather near five springs. It is dedicated to the British and German airmen who died in crashes on the hill in World War II. The direct line from the monument to Abdon Burf is wet and dull. A much better line can be found further west which is drier and retains the views westwards.

The five Springs

Alternative route

Clee Burf

Radio Aerials

The triangulation point on
Abdon Burf.

Relics of the old mineral
workings on Abdon Burf.

UPPER EARNSTREY FARM to HOPESCROSS

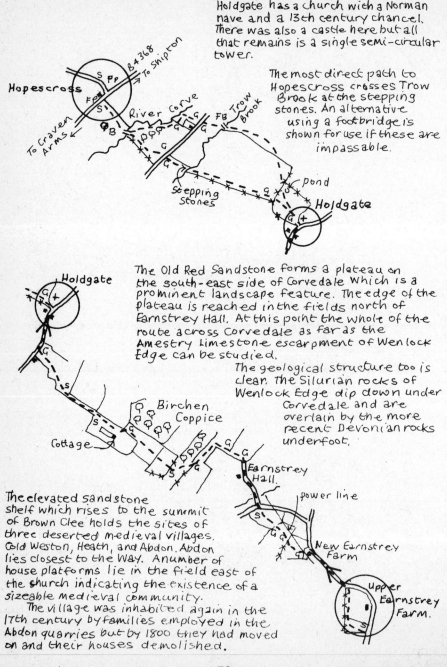

Holdgate has a church with a Norman nave and a 13th century chancel. There was also a castle here but all that remains is a single semi-circular tower.

The most direct path to Hopescross crosses Trow Brook at the stepping stones. An alternative using a footbridge is shown for use if these are impassable.

The Old Red Sandstone forms a plateau on the south-east side of Corvedale which is a prominent landscape feature. The edge of the plateau is reached in the fields north of Earnstrey Hall. At this point the whole of the route across Corvedale as far as the Amestry Limestone escarpment of Wenlock Edge can be studied.

The geological structure too is clear. The Silurian rocks of Wenlock Edge dip down under Corvedale and are overlain by the more recent Devonian rocks underfoot.

The elevated sandstone shelf which rises to the summit of Brown Clee holds the sites of three deserted medieval villages. Cold Weston, Heath, and Abdon. Abdon lies closest to the Way. A number of house platforms lie in the field east of the church indicating the existence of a sizeable medieval community.

The village was inhabited again in the 17th century by families employed in the Abdon quarries but by 1800 they had moved on and their houses demolished.

Holdgate.

The view across Corvedale to
Wenlock Edge from near Earnstrey Hall Farm.

LUDLOW to KNOWBURY CHURCH

Pass under the railway via the walkway which starts near a telephone kiosk in Sheet Road. The walkway enters a housing development which has no street names. Turn right at No 62, then along the footpath by No 54. This ends in a field which is crossed to Dark Lane.

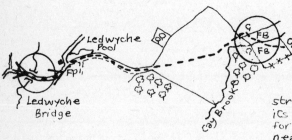

Walk 100 yards north along Dark Lane. Take the stile by the gate and walk downhill past two trees. Cross another stile and a final field to the Ludlow by-pass.

A pleasant farm track runs alongside Ledwyche Pool and ends at a large field. Knowbury Church, if it can be seen, acts as a good landmark to aim for. Otherwise strike across the field to its highest point, then aim for the wooden fence near Cay Brook.

The route from the bridge across Cay Brook to Knowbury Church presents some problems. The first of the farm tracks is encountered without difficulty. At the second farm track, the wire fence is crossed. The stile in the corner of the next field is not obvious and there is a deep ditch on the southside. The line of the path across the larger field beyond the ditch was formerly defined by hedgerows which have now gone. The stile at the stream comes into view within 220 yards when walking on a westerly line.

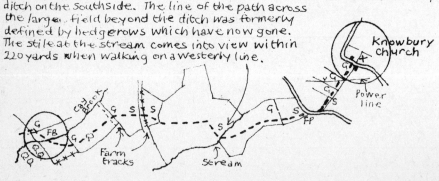

Corvedale and Brown Clee.

Wilderhope Manor.

PILGRIM'S COTTAGE to PRESTHOPE.

At Presthope the Way strikes the crest of the Wenlock limestone escarpment. The Wenlock limestones were laid down in shallow coastal waters mostly as coral reefs. The limestone averages about 100 feet in thickness and makes a continuous wooded escarpment which is one of the most beautiful features of the Shropshire landscape.

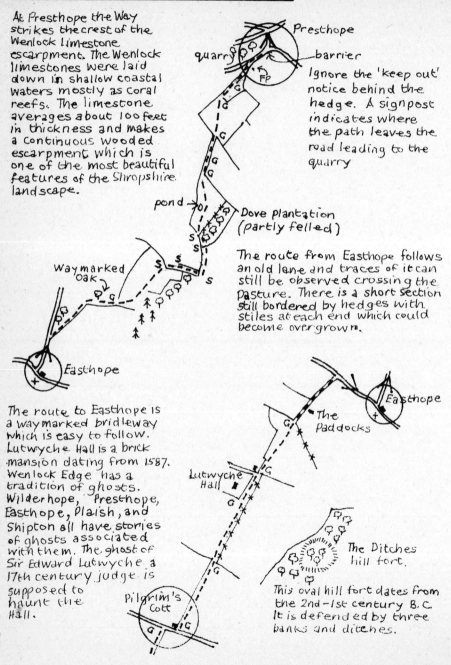

Ignore the 'keep out' notice behind the hedge. A signpost indicates where the path leaves the road leading to the quarry

The route from Easthope follows an old lane and traces of it can still be observed crossing the pasture. There is a short section still bordered by hedges with stiles at each end which could become overgrown.

The route to Easthope is a waymarked bridleway which is easy to follow. Lutwyche Hall is a brick mansion dating from 1587. Wenlock Edge has a tradition of ghosts. Wilderhope, Presthope, Easthope, Plaish, and Shipton all have stories of ghosts associated with them. The ghost of Sir Edward Lutwyche, a 17th century judge, is supposed to haunt the Hall.

This oval hill fort dates from the 2nd–1st century B.C. It is defended by three banks and ditches.

80

PRESTHOPE to MUCH WENLOCK

The footpath joins an unsurfaced track which descends eastwards to join the Church Stretton road on the outskirts of Much Wenlock. This approach to the town is probably the best. The High Street starts opposite the Gaskell Arms. It is an attractive street lined with two storey cottages and some attractive half-timbered buildings.

The path emerges from the wood at a point which overlooks ugly limestone quarries. It then picks a line between woodland and a wire fence on the brink of the quarry face. The distant view westwards across Apedale provides some compensation for the desecration close at hand. Much of the interest at close quarters lies directly underfoot. The calcareous soil produces a variety of wild flowers. A list of August flowering plants may be of interest:-

Wild strawberry
Black Knapweed.
St. John's wort
Scabious
Ragwort
Campanula

The route leaves the B4371 at a wicket gate and descends the Apedale face of Wenlock Edge between the banks of an old sunken way. Two large yews are passed and then the path joins a bridleway which contours through Blakeway Coppice to a second wicket. After 100 yards the path passes between two straight oaks. Look next for the waymark which points to the line of ascent out of the wood.

81

Much Wenlock, The Guildhall.

Holy Trinity Church.

The church has a plaque in memory of Dr. Broskes a local doctor and Greek scholar. He founded the Wenlock Olympian Society which held its first games in 1850. In 1867 he formed a National Olympic Association. A further twenty-nine years passed before the first international olympic games were held.

MUCH WENLOCK to IRONBRIDGE

East of Spring Cottage the Way joins
Benthall Edge Nature Trail near its mid
point. It is more direct to follow the
numbered posts in reverse order

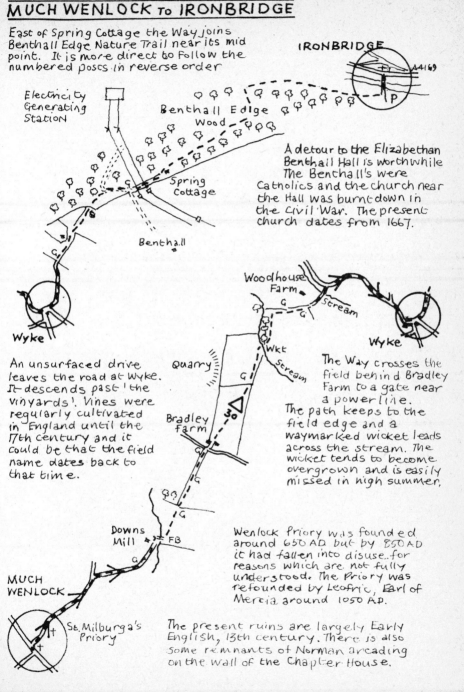

IRONBRIDGE

A detour to the Elizabethan
Benthall Hall is worthwhile.
The Benthall's were
Catholics and the church near
the Hall was burnt down in
the Civil War. The present
church dates from 1667.

An unsurfaced drive
leaves the road at Wyke.
It descends past 'the
vinyards'. Vines were
regularly cultivated
in England until the
17th century and it
could be that the field
name dates back to
that time.

The Way crosses the
field behind Bradley
Farm to a gate near
a power line.
The path keeps to the
field edge and a
waymarked wicket leads
across the stream. The
wicket tends to become
overgrown and is easily
missed in high summer.

Wenlock Priory was founded
around 650 AD but by 850 AD
it had fallen into disuse for
reasons which are not fully
understood. The Priory was
refounded by Leofric, Earl of
Mercia around 1050 AD.

The present ruins are largely Early
English, 13th century. There is also
some remnants of Norman arcading
on the wall of the Chapter House.

Much Wenlock,
Raynald's Mansion.

St. Milburga's Priory.

Main route :
IRONBRIDGE to WEM
38 miles.

Ironbridge.

The Way crosses the Severn via Abraham Darby's famous
bridge which has become one of the most well-known
monuments to the early industrial revolution.

IRONBRIDGE to THE WREKIN

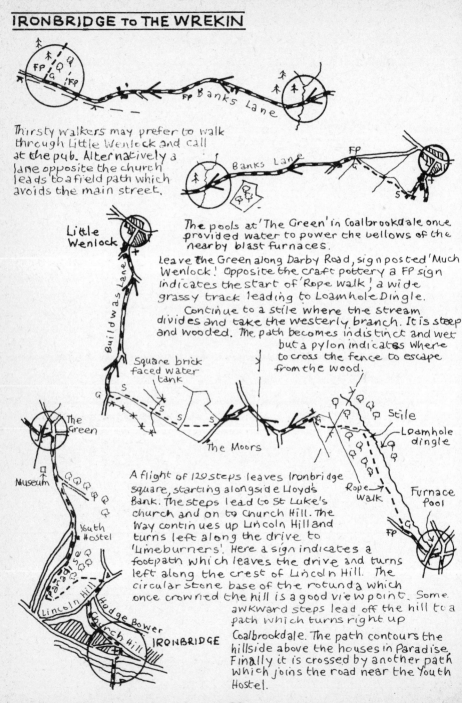

Thirsty walkers may prefer to walk through Little Wenlock and call at the pub. Alternatively a lane opposite the church leads to a field path which avoids the main street.

The pools at 'The Green' in Coalbrookdale once provided water to power the bellows of the nearby blast furnaces.

Leave the Green along Darby Road, signposted 'Much Wenlock'. Opposite the craft pottery a FP sign indicates the start of 'Rope walk', a wide grassy track leading to Loamhole Dingle.

Continue to a stile where the stream divides and take the westerly branch. It is steep and wooded. The path becomes indistinct and wet but a pylon indicates where to cross the fence to escape from the wood.

A flight of 120 steps leaves Ironbridge square, starting alongside Lloyd's Bank. The steps lead to St Luke's church and on to Church Hill. The Way continues up Lincoln Hill and turns left along the drive to 'Limeburners'. Here a sign indicates a footpath which leaves the drive and turns left along the crest of Lincoln Hill. The circular stone base of the rotunda which once crowned the hill is a good viewpoint. Some awkward steps lead off the hill to a path which turns right up Coalbrookdale. The path contours the hillside above the houses in Paradise. Finally it is crossed by another path which joins the road near the Youth Hostel.

Map labels: Banks Lane, FP, Little Wenlock, Buildwas Lane, Square brick faced water tank, The Green, The Moors, Museum, Youth Hostel, Paradise, Lincoln Hill, Hodge Bower, Church Hill, IRONBRIDGE, Stile, Loamhole dingle, Rope walk, Furnace Pool

The Square, Ironbridge.

The Market House and neighbouring buildings were built just after the Bridge in the 1760's. For its time it was a nice piece of urban planning.

Cast iron fire-hydrant on Church Hill.

It is the smallest 'listed building' passed on the Way.

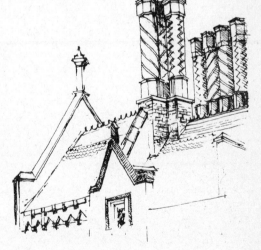

The Orchard, Church Hill.

The decorative chimneys typify the exhuberance displayed in the town's Victorian buildings. This house was once the home of Captain Matthew Webb who became the first man to swim the English Channel.

WREKIN PROSPECTS.

View north over Ercall Hill.
The hill is scarred by quarries
which expose light-coloured
Cambrian quartzite.

Imagine a glacier lying on the flat plain to the
north and the town of Telford submerged by
a glacial lake lapping the 91m contour of the
hill.

The Needle's Eye
Former volcanic lavas outcrop as small
crags near the summit. This is the largest.

View south to the Severn Gorge.
The power station marks the position of
the gorge. It is the former overflow
channel of the glacial lake which diverted
the River Severn from its former course
northwards to the
Irish Sea.

Great care is needed on this busy section of the A5.

The Wrekin is composed of some of the oldest rocks in the world. The highest part of the hill consists of rhyolitic lava, a rock which is similar in composition to granite.

The summit has been subjected to weathering through aeons of time. It once stood as an island in a dead salt sea exposed to the fierce heat of a desert sun. Then 100 000 years ago the summit rocks were experiencing arctic conditions and lakes, formed by the melt waters of glaciers invading from the north and west lapped around the base of the hill. Today the Wrekin is a fossil landscape with its rocks greatly changed from their original character.

A5

S

S

Overley Hill

C

Aston

The farm track linking Overley Hill to the A5 is not a right of Way. The suggested line takes a footpath which follows the line of the Roman Watling Street.

The view from the summit is extensive and a toposcope identifies the major landmarks. 'Heaven Gate' and 'Hell Gate' are fanciful names given to the entrances of an Iron Age hill fort.

Rifle Range

Wrekin Farm

Wrekin Course

Wrekin Cottage

Wrekin Buildings

Hell Gate

Heaven Gate

The Wrekin

Navigation Light

Needles Eye

Little Hill

FP

FP

Two signposted footpaths leave the lane west of the Shropshire County Scout Association's Camp site. The Shropshire Way takes the path furthest West. The path crosses Little Hill and takes a direct line along the crest of the hill.

The Wrekin dominates the view
southwards from where the path
crosses the railway line at
Allscott.

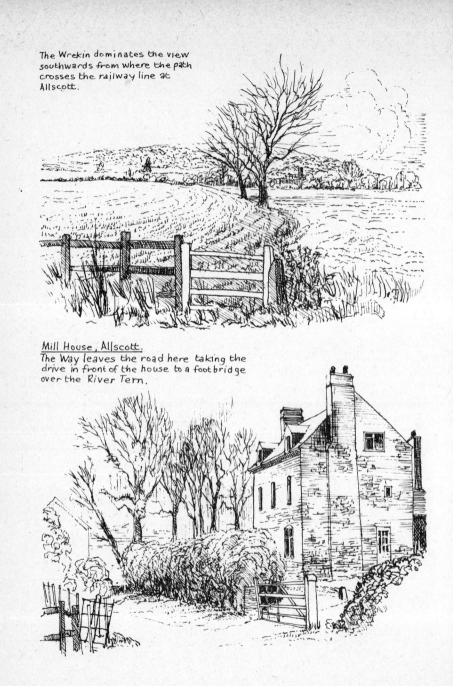

Mill House, Allscott.
The Way leaves the road here taking the
drive in front of the house to a footbridge
over the River Tern.

OVERLEY HILL TO SUGDON

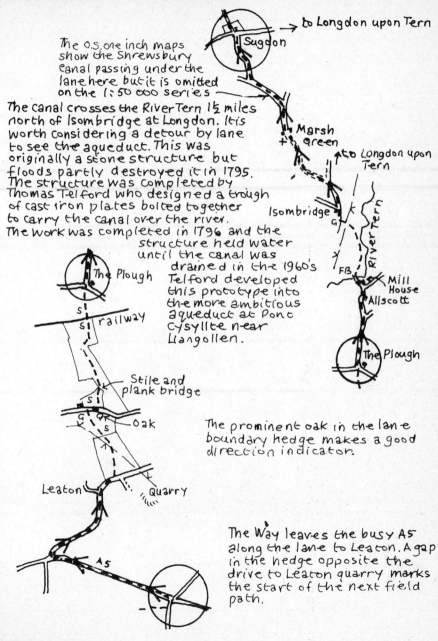

to Longdon upon Tern

Sugdon

The O.S. one inch maps show the Shrewsbury Canal passing under the lane here but it is omitted on the 1:50 000 series

Marsh green

The canal crosses the River Tern 1½ miles north of Isombridge at Longdon. It is worth considering a detour by lane to see the aqueduct. This was originally a stone structure but floods partly destroyed it in 1795. The structure was completed by Thomas Telford who designed a trough of cast iron plates bolted together to carry the canal over the river. The work was completed in 1796 and the structure held water until the canal was drained in the 1960's Telford developed this prototype into the more ambitious aqueduct at Pont Cysyllte near Llangollen.

to Longdon upon Tern

Isombridge

River Tern

FB

Mill House

Allscott

The Plough

The Plough

railway

Stile and plank bridge

Oak

The prominent oak in the lane boundary hedge makes a good direction indicator.

Leaton

Quarry

A5

The Way leaves the busy A5 along the lane to Leaton. A gap in the hedge opposite the drive to Leaton quarry marks the start of the next field path.

Telford's aqueduct, Longdon-on-Tern.

High Ercall.

SUGDON TO HIGH ERCALL

The Way leaves the village westwards along Park Road.

The church of St. Michael was severely damaged during the Civil War. Even so, much of the original medieval church has survived.

The Duke of Cleveland

Hall

High Ercall

B6062

FP

The Hall adjacent to the church withstood a year long siege during 1645-6. Nothing now remains of the moat and drawbridge which were once part of the original defences. The arcade of four semi-circular arches must also have been part of a range of buildings which once stood between the Hall and the church.

The lane from the church to the centre of the village passes an oak tree standing in a triangle of land. The tree is known as the gospel oak since it became the meeting place of Primitive Methodists some 150 years ago.

Shirlowe Cottages

oak

Wkt

to Longdon upon Tern

Sugdon

The green lane which leaves the T-junction at Sugdon ends at a gate. The path takes to the edge of the field and follows a wire fence to a conifer windbreak. The line is then fixed by the hedgrows. High Ercall church can be seen in the distance. Set amid trees on rising ground it makes a good direction indicator.

HIGH ERCALL TO MUCKLETON

Iron was once forged in the Tern and Roden valleys. An early 18th century forge was found at Wytheford but no obvious trace of it remains today.

The path to Great Wytheford takes the drive in front of a row of cottages; then through a copse and over a footbridge. West of the bungalow a gate allows access to the next field. Walk across to join an unsurfaced lane.

A pleasant green lane ends at the road junction at Muckleton.

The large field next to the B5063 may give cause for some uncertainty. The bearing should lead to a wicket gate in the hedge adjacent to an oak.

The farm at Poynton occupies the site of a medieval chapel. A three light Perpendicular period window is set into the wall of one of the farm buildings.

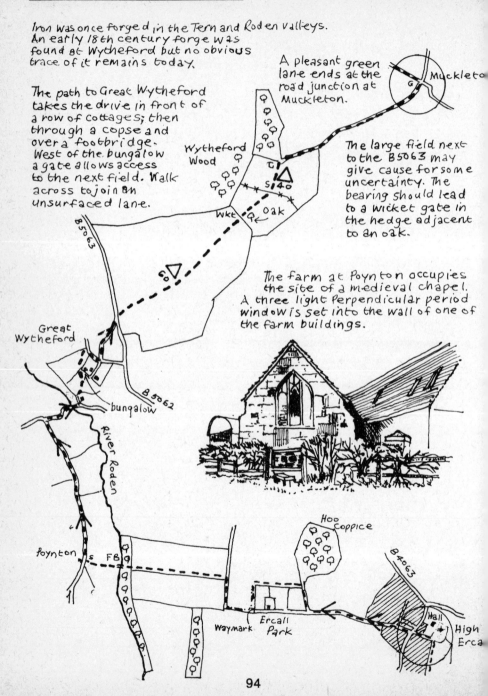

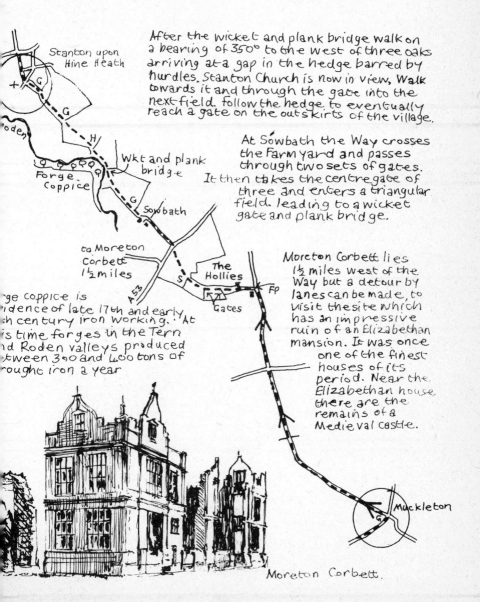

After the wicket and plank bridge walk on a bearing of 350° to the west of three oaks arriving at a gap in the hedge barred by hurdles. Stanton Church is now in view. Walk towards it and through the gate into the next field. Follow the hedge to eventually reach a gate on the outskirts of the village.

At Sowbath the Way crosses the Farm yard and passes through two sets of gates. It then takes the centre gate of three and enters a triangular field leading to a wicket gate and plank bridge.

Moreton Corbett lies 1½ miles west of the Way but a detour by lanes can be made, to visit the site which has an impressive ruin of an Elizabethan mansion. It was once one of the finest houses of its period. Near the Elizabethan house there are the remains of a Medieval castle.

ge coppice is idence of late 17th and early h century iron working. At is time forges in the Tern d Roden valleys produced tween 300 and 400 tons of rought iron a year

Moreton Corbett.

Stanton upon Hine Heath

Forge Coppice

Wkt and plank bridge

Sowbath

to Moreton Corbett 1½ miles

The Hollies

Gates

Muckleton

Lee
Brockhurst

A49

River Roden

The start of the track to
Lee Brockhurst is easily
missed. It joins the track
to Papermill Bank at an
acute angle. It runs
between outcrops of
sandstone and finally
emerges from the
wood as a wide green
lane. The lane gives
pleasant open views
north-eastwards to
the wooded hills of
Weston Heath and
Hawkstone Park.

A mature beech tree stands
near a field gate to confirm the
line. The next objective is two
lime trees. The path then
keeps to the edge of a conifer
plantation and crosses a fence
to join the cottage drive.

The Way leaves the lane from Stanton some
25 yards past the last house on the left.
It crosses a large field to a gate near the
river then follows the line of the hedge to
rejoin the lane near Harcourt Mill. Walk
the lane for some 250 yards to a stile
or use the gate a little further on. Walk
on the compass bearing to strike the exit.

Stanton-upon-Hine Heath has connections
with the novelist Mary Webb who spent
some of her childhood years at Harcourt
Manor.

Lee Brockhurst.

The stiles at the conifer plantatio
before Papermill Bank may be
difficult to locate.

Papermill
Bank

Stiles

Cott.

Harcourt
Park

Two lime
trees

beech

Harcour
Mano

350

Harcourt
Mill

Stanton
upon Hine Heath

LEE BROCKHURST TO WEM.

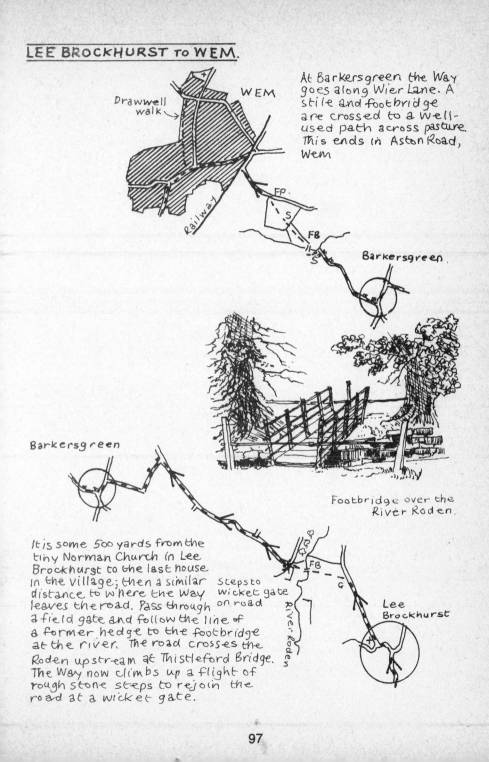

WEM

Drawwell walk →

Railway

At Barkersgreen the Way goes along Wier Lane. A stile and footbridge are crossed to a well-used path across pasture. This ends in Aston Road, Wem

FP.
S
FB
S

Barkersgreen

Barkersgreen

Footbridge over the River Roden.

It is some 500 yards from the tiny Norman Church in Lee Brockhurst to the last house in the village; then a similar distance to where the Way leaves the road. Pass through a field gate and follow the line of a former hedge to the footbridge at the river. The road crosses the Roden upstream at Thistleford Bridge. The Way now climbs up a flight of rough stone steps to rejoin the road at a wicket gate.

Steps to wicket gate on road

River Roden

FB

G

Lee Brockhurst

Shropshire Way Rambles

Some walkers may prefer to take day rambles along sections of the Way rather than walk it continuously. The following outline routes cover different sections of the Way and will give enjoyable day walks. Some of the walks are circular while others make use of the more frequent bus services.

WEM

This circular walk based on Wem involves some walking on quiet lanes between Grinshill and Stanton on Hine Heath. The circuit takes in the attractive summit of Grinshill and passes the ruined Elizabethan mansion at Moreton Corbett.
Wem - Tilley Green - Grinshill - Moreton Corbett - Stanton on Hine Heath - Wem. 12½ miles.

THE LONG MYND

The Long Mynd offers open moorland walking which make it one of the most attractive sections of the Shropshire Way. The usual routes onto it go via the steep valleys cut into its eastern flank. The Shropshire Way crosses the Long Mynd from north to south and these rambles based upon the Way offer different perspectives from those encountered on the popular routes. There is a frequent bus service along the A49 linking the towns of Shrewsbury, Church Stretton and Ludlow. (Midland Red 955/6). The suggested rambles start and finish on the A49 to enable this bus service to be used either for the outward or return journey.
Shrewsbury - Bayston Hill - Lyth Hill - Wilderley Hill - Robin Hood's Butts - Batch Valley - All Stretton. 14 miles.

Craven Arms - Sibdon Carwood - Hopesay Hill - Wart Hill - Edgton - Plowden - Pole Bank - Church Stretton. 14 miles.

Church Stretton makes a good centre for circular rambles based on the Shropshire Way. For discerning walkers, Townbrook Hollow leading up from the start of the Rectory Woods Nature Trail makes a quieter alternative than Cardingmill Valley for reaching the top of the Mynd.
Church Stretton - Townbrook Hollow - Pole Bank - Shooting Box - Priory Cottage - Coates - Adstone Hill - Stanbatch Cottage - Gliding Club - Pole Cottage - Ashes Hollow - Little Stretton. 12 miles.

Church Stretton - Cardingmill Valley - Robin Hood's Butts - Ratlinghope - Bridges - Coates - Return by reversing first part of last route. 13 miles
          Return by continuing by last part of previous route. 14½ miles.

THE ONNY VALLEY

The River Onny flows through a straight channel which was cut through the Silurian limestones of Wenlock Edge by glacier meltwater. It emerges into the wide pastoral valley of the Teme near Ludlow. The next ramble reflects these contrasts; passing first, the unique fortified manor house at Stokesay, set amid forested limestone hills; then crossing to the tiny village of Stanton Lacy on the River Corve before entering Ludlow on the line of the Teme.

Craven Arms - Stokesay - Onibury - Stanton Lacy - Ludlow. 9 miles.

THE STIPERSTONES

The ridge of The Stiperstones, strewn with frost-shattered quartzite scree, bilberry and heather is almost mountainous in character. It is deservedly popular with ramblers who can enjoy some mild scrambles on the several rocky outcrops. Super striders could combine the Long Mynd and Stiperstones in a continuous walk, but more sedentary strollers like me might prefer to start from Bridges.

Bridges - Stiperstones - Linley Hill - Norbury - Wentnor - Adstone Hill - Bridges. 12 miles.

THE CLEE HILLS

The Clee Hills are the highest hills in Shropshire and they present distinct and shapely outlines from all points of the compass. The desecrations of past mineral workings are, today, less of an eyesore than the telecommunications and radar aerials which have been placed on the summits. This aside, they are hills which provide links with man's history from earliest times and for this reason alone, they are worth exploring. The bus service from Ludlow to Birmingham (Midland Red X96), passes through the village of Clee Hill. It is possible to alight here and reach the summit of Titterstone Clee and return along the Shropshire Way to Ludlow.

Clee Hill - Titterstone Clee - Angel Bank - Knowbury - Lower Ledwyche - Ludlow. 9 miles.

A circular ramble on the north side of Titterstone Clee can be started from The Three Horseshoes Inn on the B4364 near Burwarton.

Three Horseshoes - Wheathill - Bromdon - Cleetongate - Titterstone Clee - Callowgate - Knapp Farm - Newton - Three Horseshoes. 10 miles.

The Shropshire Way crosses the road through Corvedale at Hopescross. The Seven Stars is a clearly signed hostelry which marks the start of the next ramble.

The Seven Stars - Broadstone - Tugford - Heath Chapel - Clee St. Margaret - Nordybank - Clee Burf - Abdon Burf - Earnstrey Hall - Holdgate - Hopescross. 12½ miles.

WENLOCK EDGE

The next ramble uses less than two miles of the Shropshire Way, but the footpaths and bridleways which cross Wenlock Edge are a delight and the chance to explore them should not be missed. The proposed start for the following is, again, near the Seven Stars at Hopescross.
The Seven Stars - Shropshire Way to Rowe Lane then on road used as public path and footpath to Beambridge - Millichope Park - Munslow - Little London - Wetmoor Farm - Roman Bank - Wilderhope - Shropshire Way to Hopescross. 11 miles.

IRONBRIDGE

Ironbridge, in recent years, has seen changes which have improved the town's amenities. The changes reflect the growing awareness of the importance of the town as an early industrial centre. It is a fascinating place to explore and the two walks outlined here serve only to point to further possibilities.
The Wolverhampton to Shrewsbury bus (Midland Red 892/3) can be taken from the Tontine Hotel to Overley. The Shropshire Way can then be followed back to Ironbridge.
Overley Hill - The Wrekin - Little Wenlock - The Moors - Loamhole Dingle - Coalbrookdale - Lincoln Hill - Ironbridge. 10½ miles.

An interesting circular ramble which can be started either at the car park on the south side of the Iron Bridge or at Much Wenlock is:-
Iron Bridge - Benthall Edge - Wyke - Woodhouse Farm - Bradley Farm - Much Wenlock - Arlescott Farm - Posenhall - Benthall Hall - Iron Bridge. 9 miles.

ACCOMMODATION

The section of the Way south of Shrewsbury is well-served both by Youth Hostels and Bed and Breakfast accommodation. The Youth Hostels Association Handbook and the Ramblers' Association Bed and Breakfast Guide are useful sources of reference. The north of the County has less accommodation but several farms on, or near, the Roden Valley section of the route offer Bed and Breakfast accommodation. Camping sites can be found at Lower Darnford and Wentnor on the western side of the Long Mynd and on the B4364 near Wheathill. The Camping Club of Great Britain also has a site at Ebury Hill near Shrewsbury.

TRANSPORT

Wem, Shrewsbury, and Ludlow each have main line railway stations. Good bus services connect Ludlow and Shrewsbury with Birmingham and Hereford. Ironbridge and Telford also have bus services to Wolverhampton and Birmingham. Local bus services to other places on or near the Way are very infrequent. The following companies operate local services.

* **Clun Valley Motor Services,**
Coach Garage, Newcastle,
Craven Arms, Shropshire.

For Clun - Bishops Castle
Clun - Craven Arms
Clun - Shrewsbury
Clun - Ludlow

Crosville Motor Services,
Crane Wharf, Chester.

For Whitchurch - Wem area

Midland Red (North) Ltd,
Delta Way, Longford Road,
Cannock, Staffs. WS11 3XB

For South Shropshire

Salopia Saloon Coaches Ltd,
Green End, Whitchurch,
Shropshire.

For Whitchurch - Wem - Shrewsbury
area

* **Valley Motor Services Ltd,**
Harley Jenkins Street,
Bishops Castle, Shropshire.

For Bishops Castle - Shrewsbury
Bishops Castle - Ludlow

* These companies supply their timetables free on receipt of an S.A.E. The other companies make a charge and Midland Red only provide timetables to personal callers.

PLACES OF INTEREST

    The list is restricted to places on the route or those involving a detour of less than a half-mile. Travellers willing to deviate further from the route will find many more by consulting tourist information centres.

	Grid Ref.	Opening Times
Benthall Hall	657 026	
* Haughmond Abbey	542 152	
Ironbridge Gorge Museum		
Coalbrokdale Furnace	667 047	Apr.-Oct. daily 10.00-18.00
Severn Warehouse	668 036	Nov.-Mar. daily 10.00-17.00
* Ludlow Castle	508 745	
* Moreton Corbett Castle	561 231	
Rowley House Museum, Shrewsbury	491 123	
Shrewsbury Castle	492 128	Good Fri.-Oct.
		Weekdays 10.00-17.00
		Nov. - Good Fri.
		Weekdays 10.00-16.30
* St. Milburga's Priory,	625 001	
Much Wenlock		
Stokesay Castle	436 818	Daily except Tuesday
		Summer 10.00-18.00
		Winter 10.00-16.30
Wilderhope Manor	546 929	Apr.-Sept. Wed. only
		14.30-17.00

* Opening times: May-Sept. Weekdays 09.30-19.00. Sundays 14.00-19.00.
                      Mar.,Apr. Oct. Weekdays 09.30-17.30.
                                Sundays 14.00-16.00.
                      Nov.-Feb. Weekdays 09.30-17.30. Sundays 14.30-16.00.

The opening times given were correct at January 1983 but may be subject to alteration.

SELECTED BOOK LIST

Carr, Rev. E.D. : A Night in the Snow. Onny Press
Dickens, G. : A Literary Guide to Shropshire. Shropshire Libraries
Earp, J.R. and Hains, B.A. : The Welsh Borderland. H.M.S.O.
Edmonds, F.H. and Oakley, K.P. : The Central England District. H.M.S.O.
Hains, B.A. : The Geology of the Wenlock Edge Area. H.M.S.O.
Mattingly, A. : Tackle Rambling. Stanley Paul
Painter, K.S. : Regional Archeologies, The Severn Basin. Heinemann
Pevsner, N.: The Buildings of England, Shropshire. Penguin
Rowley, T. : The Shropshire Landscape. Hodder & Stoughton
Stamp, L.D. : Britain's Structure and Scenery. Collins
Trueman, A.E. : The Geology and Scenery of England and Wales.
Penguin

GUIDES AND LEAFLETS

Ramblers Bed and Breakfast Guide. Ramblers' Association
Richards, E.L. Ed. : Hostellers Guide to the Midland Region. Y.H.A.
Ecclestone, R. : Walks in the Severn Gorge. Ironbridge and
Coalbrookdale Society
Coalbrookdale Museum and Furnace Site. Ironbridge Gorge Museum
Trust
Benthall Edge Nature Trail. Telford Development Corporation
Country Footpaths around Broseley. Telford Development Corporation
Country Footpaths around Coalbrookdale. Telford Development Corp.
Country Footpaths around Little Wenlock. Telford Development Corp.
Country Footpaths around The Wrekin. Telford Development Corp.
Country Footpaths around Wrockwardine. Telford Development Corp.
Walks around Wem. Wem Walkers and Shropshire County Council
The Sandstone Trail. Cheshire County Council